People to Know

# Garth
# Brooks
## *Country Music Superstar*

*Laura Lee Wren*

**Enslow Publishers, Inc.**

| 40 Industrial Road | PO Box 38 |
| Box 398 | Aldershot |
| Berkeley Heights, NJ 07922 | Hants GU12 6BP |
| USA | UK |

http://www.enslow.com

**Library of Congress Cataloging-in-Publication Data**

Wren, Laura Lee.
    Garth Brooks : country music superstar / Laura Lee Wren.
       p. cm. — (People to know)
    Includes bibliographical references and index.
    ISBN 0-7660-1672-2
    1. Brooks, Garth—Juvenile literature. 2. Country musicians—United States—
Biography—Juvenile literature. [1. Brooks, Garth. 2. Musicians. 3. Country music.]
I. Title. II. Series.
    ML3930.B855 W74 2001
    782.42164'092—dc21

                    2001002396

Printed in the United States of America

10 9 8 7 6 5 4 3 2 1

**To Our Readers:**
We have done our best to make sure all Internet Addresses in this book were active and
appropriate when we went to press. However, the author and the publisher have no control over and assume no liability for the material available on those Internet sites or on
other Web sites they may link to. Any comments or suggestions can be sent by e-mail
to comments@enslow.com or to the address on the back cover.

Every effort has been made to locate all copyright holders of material used in this book.
If any errors or omissions have occurred, corrections will be made in future editions of
this book.

**Illustration Credits:** © 1998 Michelle Kramer, michkram@cinci.rr.com,
p. 77; Associated Press, pp. 4, 8, 13, 46, 49, 57, 60, 65, 89; Cindy Murphy,
1996, pp. 30, 34, 38; Photofest, pp. 11, 21, 53, 75, 90.

**Cover Illustration:** Photofest

# Contents

*Garth Brooks*

# Standing Outside the Fire

During the summer of 1985, twenty-three-year-old Garth Brooks decided it was about time the country music industry discovered him. He was ready to become a famous country music star.

Brooks realized success was not going to happen in Oklahoma, so he quit his job selling sporting goods, moved out of his Stillwater, Oklahoma, apartment, and drove east, heading for Nashville, Tennessee, the country music capital of the world.

"I begged Garth not to go," his mother remembered. She told him, "I want you to get a real job. That's why we've sent you to college."[1] But there was no stopping him.

"[I] pulled in expecting to see my name on every water tower in the place," Brooks later joked, admitting he had been naive.[2] He quickly found that Nashville was a bustling city crowded with others pursuing the same dream of becoming country music stars. "I thought this town was like Oz, and you came here and all your prayers were answered."[3]

With a tape of his recorded music in hand and the hope that he would make it big, Brooks strode into Merlin Littlefield's office at the American Society of Composers, Authors and Publishers. Rather than embracing the young man and offering him a contract, Littlefield offered this hard advice: "Go home."[4]

Brooks strode right out of the office and kept on going—all the way to Oklahoma. "I hated his guts," Brooks said. "The whole way home I cussed him."[5] He was back home within twenty-four hours. "I had burned all my bridges [back home]," he said, "and I came back a day later like a whipped pup."[6]

"It wasn't failure," his mother said, reflecting on her son's disappointment. "He just didn't know the ins and outs."[7]

At that moment, though, Brooks felt like a failure. Yet his dream would not die. Though country music was experiencing a boom in popularity, it took another year of working on his music and his self-confidence before Brooks felt ready to return to Nashville, the heart of the industry. In the spring of 1987 Brooks took the trip east again. "If you're gonna play in the big league," Brooks said, "you've gotta be where they're swingin' the bats."[8]

This time he did not go alone; he brought his band along with him. The experience of a first trip to Nashville proved just as tough on his friends, for the band soon dissolved. Brooks remained in Nashville and found small paying gigs here and there. Unpaid bills and frustration mounted. Once, Brooks sat in a parking lot on the brink of giving up. "[I was] beating my head as hard as I could because I had snapped," Brooks said.[9] Eventually, he got control of his anger, calmed down, and focused on his goal. He would be a famous country music singer. He gained new strength and determination. "He's always wanted to try to do the best he can," explained Garth's older brother Kelly. "It's just a competition with himself."[10] Garth Brooks would not let Nashville break him again.

It was a warm spring evening when Brooks's luck turned around. During a show highlighting amateur acts at the Bluebird Cafe, he waited in the dark, smoke-filled room for his turn to perform. When one of the early acts failed to show up, Brooks filled the spot. He took the stage alone with his acoustic guitar. As the spotlight shone on him, he sang clear and strong. He did not know that Lynn Shults, a Capitol Records executive, was sitting in the audience, impressed by what he heard from this young singer.

"Garth was exceptional," Shults remembered. "The bells and whistles went off."[11]

Shults was the right person to impress. He quickly offered Brooks his first record contract. Brooks was on his way to stardom.

That country boy from Oklahoma who first tasted

*The country boy from Oklahoma won hearts around the world.*

rejection in Nashville eventually won hearts the world over. From small college sing-alongs to stadium performances in front of thousands, Garth Brooks opened his arms to gather friends, new and old. He broke just about every record in the music industry, boasting a Grammy and many multiplatinum albums. During the 1990s, the Academy of Country Music declared Garth Brooks "Artist of the Decade."

# A Young Athlete

In the 1950s, Colleen Carroll was trying to make it in the country music industry. She achieved her success by performing on radio and television with Red Foley's "Ozark Jubilee" and recording a few songs for Capitol Records. Though the life of a country music star could be exciting, she and Troyal Brooks, an oil company engineer and former U.S. marine, chose a quieter life for their family. They moved from the big city of Tulsa, Oklahoma, to the flat, cowboy country of Yukon, just west of Oklahoma City. Back then, Colleen and Troyal had no way of knowing how much the country music industry would continue to affect their lives.

The Brooks family consisted of three children from

Colleen's previous marriage, one from Troyal's previous marriage, and an eighteen-month-old son, Kelly. They were blessed with another boy when Troyal Garth Brooks was born on February 7, 1962. Later, with the birth of little sister Betsy, the family was complete.

The 1960s were turbulent times. People in the United States struggled with civil rights issues, witnessed the assassination of a popular president, and watched in amazement as a man first set foot on the moon. At that time, the Brooks family flourished in the small farming community that had grown up around the Yukon Flour Mill along Route 66, America's famous highway that runs from Illinois to California. The seven children kept the house lively and full of laughter.

As the kids grew, Colleen Brooks shared her love of music with them. Many evenings were spent together in their suburban home with one person strumming a guitar, another singing old tunes, and others adding to the melody with kazoos. "We kids felt that she had cut her career short because of us," Garth later explained, "and we wanted to carry on the tradition for her."[1] That tradition was being upheld even as her young son Garth performed on stage dressed as a big Fig Newton cookie in his fourth grade talent show.

Some nights, the kids would take turns performing for their friends and family. "Garth was a ham as a kid," said his sister Betsy. "He'd do anything for the spotlight or for laughs."[2]

He did have a flair for the dramatic. One fantasy Garth would act out was the last play of a football game. Of course, it would be the Hail Mary, a long high pass flying through the air. "I catch the ball and hit the goalpost at exactly the same time," Garth remembered. He would fall to the ground, shaking violently while in his mind the crowd went crazy. "And finally, I die with the ball in my hand."[3] To Garth, those old fantasies were not strange. "The last thing you do in life, you're a winner," he explained.[4]

During the 1970s, even though his parents' choice of music was country, Garth was exposed to a variety of styles. Not only did he listen to Willie Nelson

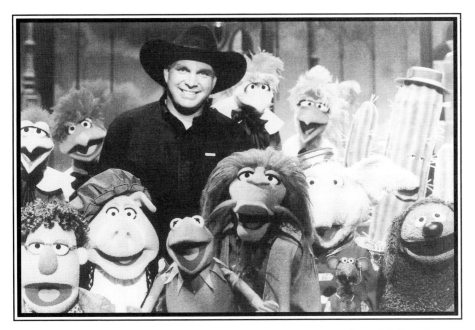

*Brooks, pictured with the Muppets, never outgrew his childhood passion for hamming it up.*

and Waylon Jennings, he was one of millions of teenage fans who hung a poster of the hard-rock group KISS on a bedroom wall. He went to a Queen concert, but also admired many quieter songwriters. "James Taylor, Dan Fogelberg, Elton John, Billy Joel—all those people are geniuses," Garth said.[5] He would teach himself songs by his favorite singers, playing first on an acoustic guitar, then on an electric guitar with an amplifier.

While music was a big part of Garth's life, it was not his main focus. He was more interested in sports. This was his father's influence. Troyal Brooks would insist that no matter which sport—football, baseball, or track and field—Garth must never give up and should always play his best. "You might be able to fool the whole world, but the Little Man Inside will know," he would say, poking Garth in the chest while teaching him the importance of conscience.[6] Garth later described his father as "thundering tenderness." He described him as having "the shortest temper . . . and the biggest heart."[7]

Young Garth tried his best on the playing fields, but he was not the most talented athlete on the team. "Athletics was a way to keep my interest in school," Garth admitted.[8] He played football quarterback and baseball outfielder, and he tried different events in track and field. He graduated from Yukon High School in 1980 with good grades and was offered a partial scholarship to Oklahoma State University, where he would compete in the javelin.

Brooks was just over six feet tall and weighed 225

*In high school and college, Garth liked sports more than music. But it was his music that would bring him to the majors one day. Here, he autographs baseballs for some Padres fans in 1999.*

pounds. His brother Kelly was already at OSU on a track scholarship, so the two roomed together in Iba Hall dormitory. Garth was able to hurl the javelin, a light metal spear, two hundred feet, and he could bench-press more than three hundred pounds.[9] While other javelin hurlers were well focused on practicing their craft, Brooks confessed, "Just hauling that . . . thing down the runway was work."[10] Still, he always tried his best and enjoyed being part of a team. Once a week the throwers would go to a restaurant that specialized in barbecued ribs. There, Garth came up with the term "power eating." "We would all go power eating together," remembered Gary Polson, an assistant coach for the track team. "Garth could put down with the big boys."[11]

While working toward a marketing degree, Brooks studied the basics, such as math and English, and also took classes in advertising and public relations. When he was not studying or working out with the track team, Brooks was often asked to perform his music at campus parties. Soon he was playing gigs at bars and pizza places around town. Sometimes, he and friends would jam together in front of the university's Student Union building until a security guard would send them back to their dorm. "Hanging out with a bunch of my buddies and playing music . . . it was some of the most fun I've ever had," Brooks later reminisced.[12]

As was the fashion of the time, Brooks wore his hair long and had a full beard and mustache. He played a wide mix of songs, varying from Willie Nelson's country style to Billy Joel's pop rock. He would even sneak in a few songs he had written himself. At the end of the night, he usually ended his shows with Don McLean's ballad "American Pie," encouraging the audience to sing along.

By his junior year, Brooks found these gigs did not pay enough to cover his college expenses, so he took a job at a sporting goods store. These were long days, but Brooks seemed to have an endless supply of energy. To unwind after work, he played guitar into the late hours with his roommate, Ty England. "We made a pact with each other that someday [we would] get back together and do duets," Brooks remembered.[13]

England believed that dream just might come true. "Country music stars were just completely out of reach in my world," he said. "But Garth's mother had made records, so I knew it was possible."[14]

One day, a childhood friend from Yukon, Mickey Weber, visited Brooks on campus. They went for a drive, along with another friend, and the three relaxed in friendly camaraderie, the fresh Oklahoma air rushing past the car windows. Suddenly, their car was crushed under a flatbed truck. Weber flew through the windshield up to his chest, and the third friend would later need facial surgery for his injuries. Brooks had been alone in the backseat. "He got his hat crushed," Weber recalled. "That was about it."[15] It was fortunate that all three survived the crash, and it was one of the first signs of the good luck that would continually follow Brooks.

Not long after the accident, Garth was on another car ride, this time with his father. As they drove along, Garth flipped through stations on the radio, searching for something he and his father could both enjoy. He stopped when a new song captured his attention, and it went straight to his heart. The song was "Unwound," performed by the new country singer George Strait. "I became a George wannabe and imitator for the next seven years," Brooks said.[16]

Sports became less and less important to Brooks, while music took on a larger role. But in his senior year, when Brooks did not make the Big Eight track and field finals, he still felt the disappointment. His trainer told him, "Now you can get on with what you're supposed to be doing."[17] At the time, the disappointed athlete had no idea what that would be. What would his future hold?

# Pursuing a Dream

Garth Brooks continued to take college classes during the day. At night, he supported himself by playing gigs and working at the sporting goods store. Occasionally he took on various odd jobs, like delivering pizzas. Another of those jobs was being a bouncer at a nightclub called Tumbleweeds. He was in charge of keeping rambunctious people under control. One night, he was called into the ladies' rest room for assistance. There stood an attractive blonde, dressed all in black from felt cowboy hat down to pointed-toe boots. Her fist was stuck in the plywood wall.

While Garth helped the woman free her hand, she explained that in a confrontation with another woman over an old boyfriend, "I missed."[1] He learned that her name was Sandy Mahl and that she was a fellow OSU student.

Soon after, Garth and Sandy could be seen walking around campus, holding hands. They went to see *Starman* and other movies together. It was not long before the two fell in love.

In December 1984, Brooks graduated from college with a bachelor's degree in advertising. Rather than look for a job in that field, he told his mother he thought he might move to Nashville and try to make it as a country singer.

Garth handed his mother the tassel from his graduation cap and asked for her blessing to pursue a music career. "I never gave him my blessing," she said, but she did tell him, "I'll pray for you."[2]

Brooks made a demo tape of some of his songs in a Stillwater recording studio, hoping to prove his talent to a music business executive. His friends in Stillwater passed around a hat and helped come up with enough money for Brooks to try his luck at stardom. In the summer of 1985, he gave up his apartment, quit his job at Dupree's sporting goods store, and headed for Nashville, full of high hopes. "I [imagined] you'd . . . flip open your guitar case, play a song, and someone would . . . tell you, 'Come into the studio right quick, son, we got ten songs we want you to cut.'"[3] He even dreamed of seeing his name painted on his hometown's water tower.

His dream was quickly shattered. "I had thought the world was waiting for me," said Brooks, "but there's nothing colder than reality."[4]

Reality came from a meeting with Merlin Littlefield, director of ASCAP, the American Society of Composers, Authors and Publishers. After introducing himself to the secretary, Brooks was ushered into an office and seated in front of a large mahogany desk. The executive listened to Brooks's demo tape, and then was blunt. "You [will] either starve as a songwriter or get five people together and . . . starve as a band."[5] He advised Brooks to return home.

Though he hated the man's message, Brooks spent the night in a hotel room, staring at the ceiling and thinking about Littlefield's harsh description of the competitive music business. Brooks took the man's advice and was back in Oklahoma within twenty-four hours. He returned to the landlord, his boss, his girlfriend, his family, and his friends. All of them knew that Brooks had expected to return a star. No one gave him a hard time. He was able to get his apartment back, his job at Dupree's, even his girlfriend, Sandy. The hometown hero had learned a lesson in humility.

Brooks spent the next year assembling a new band. He recruited a bass player, Tom Skinner. They had met back at OSU's Student Union, and Tom now worked at a local post office. Brooks found a lead guitarist, Jed Lindsay, who used to play in a rock band at Tumbleweeds, where Brooks had been a bouncer. Garth even approached a neighbor, Matt O'Meilia, a drummer who considered himself a rock musician. O'Meilia took a bit more convincing. "I imagined myself in a cowboy hat, bolo tie, and a leather belt with my name on it, trying to beat my bass drum wearing cowboy boots," O'Meilia said when describing his decision to join up with the new band.[6] Brooks eventually convinced him that their group, to be called Santa Fe, would play all types of music.

In April 1986, Santa Fe began its gig as a house band for Binks, a new club in downtown Stillwater. From a long stage raised about a foot off the floor and a mirrored backdrop, they played rock, pop, and country—whatever the crowd wanted to hear. "Never was a song requested by the audience that either Garth or Tom didn't know or hadn't at least heard," Matt O'Meilia said of the huge amount of material the band could play.[7] Tom Skinner's brother Mike joined the band, and his fiddle playing helped them add bluegrass to their variety.

Their sets included "Much Too Young (To Feel This Damn Old)," a song that Brooks had written with his friend Randy Taylor, who was a rodeo rider. The bar crowd responded to that original song with cheers and applause. During breaks between sets, while the rest of the band headed out the back door for a cigarette break, Brooks would go out into the crowd, shaking hands, telling jokes, and making friends.

The band grew in popularity, and quickly booked more and more dates. They managed to take one weekend off from their busy schedule. On May 24, 1986, Garth and Sandy were married in a small wedding ceremony held in Sandy's hometown, Owasso, Oklahoma. "They made a great team," said their friend Jon Small. "I watched them two-step together, and it blew me away."[8] The newlyweds

*Garth and Sandy Brooks*

moved into O'Meilia's house when he moved back in with his parents. It was a bright lemon-yellow color, standing out among the mostly white A-frame homes in the neighborhood.

All summer and through the rest of the year, Santa Fe performed at local clubs, often opening for bigger acts, such as new country recording star Dwight Yoakam. They performed at Tulsa City Limits, one of the best country music and dance clubs in America. Brooks's sister Betsy occasionally joined the band onstage, singing and playing guitar, as did Ty England, Brooks's old OSU friend.

By the time New Year's Eve rolled around, Brooks was ready to give Nashville another try, this time with his band. The rest of the band members agreed to pack up their families and move to the city of opportunity. All except Matt O'Meilia, the drummer. It was not the path he wanted to take. He remained with the band until they found another drummer, Troy Jones. Santa Fe's last Oklahoma performance was at Norm's Country Ballroom. Norm Brown introduced the band, telling the audience that the band would soon be heading out to Nashville. "It's gonna be the last time you'll see a band this good in a li'l ol' honky-tonk like this," he announced.[9] In the spring of 1987, Santa Fe was ready to make its move.

The first step was finding a place to live. A five-bedroom brick house in Hendersonville, just outside Nashville, fit the bill. All five band members, two wives, a child, and the Brooks's Siberian husky, Sasha, filled the two-story home. Next was the search for jobs. Garth and Sandy both started working at a boot shop near Rivergate Mall, selling cowboy boots. Finally, it was time to focus on music once again.

By now, country music had begun its rise in popularity. Twenty-two-year-old Randy Travis was attracting younger audiences to the genre, as were other stars such as Lorrie Morgan, Reba McEntire, and the Judds. Country Music Television followed its rock predecessor, MTV, and showed off the young, good-looking musicians on cable television. "Videos on TNN and CMT . . . can create that all-important visual image that's the foundation for success," said agent Tony Conway.[10] Because of this country music boom, there was a lot of interest in new talent.

Still, the road to the top was not without bumps. After only two months, the members of Santa Fe became discouraged. It did not prove easy for the friends with various personalities to live in the same home. They decided to dissolve the band. Garth had his doubts too, but Sandy encouraged him to stick it out. "I'm not makin' this trip every year," she told him. "Either we're diggin' in, or we're goin' home for good."[11] They dug in.

For the next year, Brooks concentrated on songwriting. In between selling boots, he wrote "Not Counting You." He met other songwriters, including Stephanie Brown and Kent Blazy, and they collaborated on many songs with emotional, heartfelt lyrics. He met other singers hoping to break into the industry, such as Billy Dean and Trisha Yearwood. He played at small clubs outside Nashville, and recorded demo tapes of new songs. People started talking about the big man with the incredible voice who sang with such intensity.

Even so, success was not coming fast enough. Brooks would often become frustrated and impatient, especially when struggling to pay the bills. One night, Brooks sat in the parking lot of a fire station. "[I was] beating my head as hard as I could [with] Sandy screaming at me to quit. I was crying, she was crying. I calmed down, and we went back home," he said.[12]

Brooks may have been down, but he never gave up. His persistence paid off. He persuaded the management team of Bob Doyle and Pam Lewis to sign him as their first client. He was then taken on by booking agent Joe Harris. Together, their goal was to make Brooks a star.

After recording a professional demo tape, Brooks posed in his jeans, boots, and cowboy hat for publicity photos. Lewis found it easy to write a short bio about Brooks's background. "He referred to himself as a human jukebox," Lewis said. "He had a unique voice . . . captivating blue eyes and a nice smile."[13] These complete packages of demo tapes, pictures, and biographical information were sent to many record companies.

Yet, even with a promotion team backing him, Brooks still met rejection. Every single record company turned him down. One executive, Jimmy Bowen, thought Brooks was "impressive" but did not sound like "*real* country."[14] However, the days of rejection were about to change.

The Nashville Entertainment Association was sponsoring a show at the Bluebird Cafe in May 1988. The Doyle/Lewis Management Company had submitted Garth Brooks's audition tape, and he was chosen from dozens of others to perform along with top artists. He was to go onstage later in the show, after the audience had been warmed up. But as Brooks leisurely waited for his turn onstage, enjoying the first performance of another musician, he was asked to move up to second in the show to fill in for someone who was late.

Meanwhile, Capitol Records executive Lynn Shults was looking for a place to sit in the crowd. He was always interested in finding new talent, though he did not expect anything special that evening.

Garth Brooks took the stage with only his acoustic guitar. He closed his eyes, took a deep breath and let his voice fill with emotion. He sang to the crowd as if sharing a personal story with them alone. The song was "If Tomorrow Never Comes," one he had written with Kent Blazy.

The intense emotion could be felt by everyone in the room. "It was a magical moment," Shults said. "His vocal performance and [the] magnetism of his personality connected with people who didn't even know who Garth Brooks was."[15]

Capitol Records immediately offered Garth Brooks $10,000 to record four songs. He had his first record deal. The dream was becoming reality.

# 4

# The Dance

During the Christmas holiday season of 1988, Garth Brooks's booking agent, Joe Harris, received a desperate plea from the sheriff of Cleveland, Tennessee. Harris's minister was about to be evicted from his home, along with his wife and children, because he owed $4,800 in back rent. No one wants to evict a family from their home, especially just before Christmas, and the sheriff had hoped Harris could somehow help.[1]

After some quick phone calls, the money was raised. Harris asked Garth Brooks to go along with him to offer the family the money. Perhaps because he had just received his advance from Capitol Records, and because he had so recently felt the same despair from overdue bills, Brooks did not hesitate to add $1,000 to the pot. This was only the first of many demonstrations of Brooks's charitable heart.

Meanwhile, Allen Reynolds, the producer of hits for country star Kathy Mattea, was looking for a male artist to work with. Manager Bob Doyle convinced Reynolds that Garth Brooks could fit the bill. After listening to his music and talking with him about his career goals, Reynolds agreed to produce four of Brooks's songs for Capitol.

Part of Reynolds's job was to bring together musicians for a studio recording. He chose six new band members to support his new artist: Mike Chapman on bass, Milton Sledge on drums, Bobby Wood on keyboard, Mark Casstevens on acoustic guitar, and Chris Leuzinger on electric guitar. After hearing the four recorded songs, Capitol decided to go ahead and record an entire album. Back to the studio they went, this time adding Bruce Bouton on steel guitar and the soulful fiddle playing of Rob Hajacos, who had helped Brooks on the demo tape of "Much Too Young (To Feel This Damn Old)."

Once the recording was finished, Brooks would have to wait until the album's release in the spring to find out the country's reaction to his music. In the meantime, he would continue playing gigs. For this he needed a touring band.

True to his word, he called his old friends in Oklahoma. The first call was to his college roommate, Ty England. Years before, they had made a pact to call each other if one of them ever hit the big time.

England, who at the time had a job selling paint, immediately agreed to join his friend. Unfortunately, because of other commitments, the only other musician from back home who could take advantage of this opportunity was keyboard and fiddle player David Gant. Joining them in the band, called Stillwater to honor Brooks's old college town, were James Garver, Steve McClure, and Mike Palmer. They rehearsed in the dark, damp basement of manager Bob Doyle's office building.

Finally, the album *Garth Brooks* was released. The song he had played to the crowds back home, "Much Too Young (To Feel This Damn Old)," could often be heard over the radio. It quickly rose to the Top 40 list of country songs, but then just as quickly left the charts.

Still, Brooks persisted. In June 1989, he performed at Fan Fair, a weeklong country music festival at the Tennessee State Fairgrounds. Then he went on the road with Stillwater. They opened for large concert acts, such as Steve Wariner, and also played at small clubs. When he performed at Tulsa City Limits in August, a crowd of friends was cheering in the audience. A reviewer wrote, "After seeing what he can do in concert, I'll go out on a limb and predict that Brooks . . . is going to be country music's Next Big Thing."[2] Much later, Brooks confessed to the critic that he had kept that review for years. "You were the only one who said that," Brooks remembered.[3]

Perhaps not everyone was so optimistic, but all the while, Brooks was gaining new fans. Audiences were treated to shows that revealed a man who would do all sorts of things onstage. He might pick out a woman from the crowd and sing a song especially for her. At clubs, he might leave the stage to join dancers on the dance floor, or jump on a table to dance and sing in the middle of the audience. After shows he would stick around to meet his fans, talking to them, shaking their hands, and signing autographs until every autograph seeker was gone. "He didn't just sign my shirt," said one fan, who had stood in line for more than an hour for an autograph. "He actually talked to me."[4] These gestures were not merely for show. They were the real Garth Brooks having fun doing what he loved. "More than anything else, Garth taught me that every fan is important," Ty England later said. "They are the reason you're out there."[5]

Word of Brooks's unique performances spread, and sales of his album grew. Suddenly, "Much Too Young" was back on the radio, and in August it reached number eight on the *Billboard* charts. Brooks had his first hit.

In September, "If Tomorrow Never Comes" was released from the same album, a tender song that proclaims the importance of telling people how you feel about them when you have the opportunity. Brooks dedicated the song to a former track coach and to a college friend who had both died in tragic accidents. "That song means a lot to me because of friends I've lost," he said.[6]

The touching lyrics must have meant a lot to many others as well, for the song raced to the number-one spot. Garth Brooks had his first major hit.

*One music critic predicted that Brooks would be "country music's Next Big Thing."*

That meant it was time to make a music video. The setting for "If Tomorrow Never Comes" is the lush, green lawn outside a Victorian house that Garth and Sandy had often admired as they drove by. In the video, Sandy plays a young woman cheerfully romping in the yard with a child while Garth sings of his worry that he has not shown them enough of his love.

*Garth Brooks* shot to number two on the country charts, just behind country star Clint Black's *Killin' Time*. The competition between the two men in cowboy hats had begun. Black later said, "I know that Garth joked about hating me when I first came out, but he thought I was too nice to hate." Black added, "Anybody who's raised in America is going to have some sense of competition."[7]

Garth Brooks fans were now discovering other songs on the album, such as "Everytime That It Rains," "Not Counting You," and a song with lyrics cowritten by Sandy, "I've Got a Good Thing Going." Critics agreed with the fans. One reviewer wrote, "Brooks . . . mak[es] a direct assault on the heartstrings, singing in a . . . tenor suitable for both serenades and bust outs."[8]

Garth would soon find that life on the road is filled with many temptations. A person who suddenly finds himself a star may have a difficult time dealing with those temptations. It is not uncommon for a celebrity to turn to a wild lifestyle, such as using drugs or alcohol. Some have been known to trash hotel rooms or assault photographers who intrude on their privacy. It might be hard to turn away the many attractive women interested in spending time with a celebrity.

That last weakness is what Sandy Brooks heard was happening to her husband while he was on the road. She was devastated, and confronted him with the rumors that he was cheating on her. "My bags were packed; my plane tickets bought," she said.[9]

That November night, while on a stage in Missouri and performing "If Tomorrow Never Comes," Brooks became choked up and had to stop singing. "I explained to the crowd what was going on, and I asked for a second chance," Brooks remembered.[10] He looked back at his band members and could see how bad they felt. He then realized how his actions had affected all of them.

After the concert, Brooks took his own advice from the song and returned to his wife. "I love her to death," Garth said of Sandy. "When I've been down [she] has given me strength."[11] By the spring of 1990, Garth and Sandy had promised each other to do everything they could to keep their marriage the most important thing in their lives. A promise was not a guarantee that all would go smoothly from then on. Like all married couples, they would work together to stay on an even course on the bumpy road ahead.

In April 1990, the Academy of Country Music held its annual awards ceremony. Brooks had been nominated for Male Vocalist of the Year, Song of the Year, and the Horizon Award, which acknowledges the most promising newcomer. He sat in the audience during that awards ceremony, which was broadcast on national television, but he never heard his name called as a winner.

Meanwhile, the public still had not had enough of the debut album. Another single was released, one that would later become one of his signature songs. When people think of Garth Brooks, they often think of "The Dance."

"The Dance" is not a traditional country music song. Yet, at the heart of most country songs is a sense of reality that tugs at the emotions. "The Dance" has that emotional pull. It emphasizes that bad things are sure to happen in one's life, but one must accept them in order to also experience the good in life. A relationship may come to a sad ending, but to avoid it one would have had to miss out on all the happiness it had brought. "He took a song with very simple lyrics and made [it] mean the whole world to people," said Ty England.[12]

In the song's video, Brooks added even more depth to the story. He sings the tender lyrics as powerful news footage of Martin Luther King, Jr., and John F. Kennedy are interwoven with film clips of actors. Musicians, including Janis Joplin and John Lennon, are shown, as well as the crew of the space shuttle *Challenger.* The video is a tribute to the many heroes whose lives were cut short.

Even as "The Dance" shot to number one on the charts, Brooks felt it was time to make some changes. He asked his brother Kelly to leave his banking job and help with the business details of his career. His childhood friend Mickey Weber agreed to become road manager. And Garth's sister Betsy joined the band,

Brooks knew how to have fun with his audience, and word of his
unique performances spread.

singing and playing bass guitar. He was surrounded with friends and family.

However, Capitol Records was also undergoing big management changes. Lynn Shults, the man who had "discovered" Garth Brooks, was no longer with the company. Now in control of Brooks's recordings was Jimmy Bowen, one of the men who had said no to Garth's audition only a year before. The first thing he did was watch Brooks perform live. He was surprised that the easygoing man who had played for him in his living room the previous year was the same person as the fiery-eyed performer making eye contact with everyone in the crowd. At one point during the show, Brooks jumped into the audience to take a baby from his mother and sing "If Tomorrow Never Comes" as a tear-jerking lullaby.

"Onstage you're this vibrant, electrifying presence," Bowen told the singer. "That's not in the album."[13] Bowen wanted another album cut right away, and this time he wanted to feel the excitement of a live performance.

Garth Brooks had achieved incredible success with only one album. In an interview, Reba McEntire tried explaining Brooks's sudden popularity. "[Many] artists can sing but [don't have] the emotion and personality that make an entertainer shine," she said. "Garth pulls it off."[14]

But after such instant success, would he be able to follow it by "pulling it off" again?

## 5

# Garth Brooks Fever

**W**hen the president of Capitol Records asks for an exciting record, that is what he is going to get. As Garth Brooks prepared to record a track for his second album, he invited close friends into the studio. In this fun, party atmosphere, he created what would become another signature song— "Friends in Low Places."

Very different from the reflective ballad that was his last hit, this song tells it like it is, plain and simple, with a touch of humor. It seemed as though the entire country could relate to the song in which Brooks proclaimed comfort in being around common, everyday people. Radio disc jockeys played it, live audiences sang along with it, and *Billboard* charts had to be adjusted each week as it rose higher and higher.

While at the country event Fan Fair in 1990, Brooks was on top of the world. His new hit was being played everywhere, his first album had just hit gold, meaning half a million copies had been sold, the new album *No Fences* was released, and the Country Music Association announced Brooks was nominated for five awards: Male Vocalist of the Year, Single of the Year ("The Dance"), Song of the Year ("If Tomorrow Never Comes"), Video of the Year ("The Dance"), and the Horizon Award, presented to a new artist who has shown the most growth in the previous year. Fans stood in line in the scorching heat to get his auto-graph, or a picture of themselves with Garth and his gold record. For hours, Brooks remained with his fans, signing autographs, taking pictures, and thank-ing them for their support.

Later, many people attended a benefit concert for children with cancer or serious blood diseases. They were there because they wanted to help the charity, and many who were not country music fans had never heard of Garth Brooks. Those who had heard of him may never have imagined he would be the guy in sweats and baseball cap, joking around with friends backstage. "He loved running up and down the steps at the amphitheater," said concert coordinator Elizabeth Oakley Norris of Brooks's actions during the afternoon sound check. "He and some of his band guys would race on the stairs. He was in great shape."[1] During the concert, however, it was his per-formance that won over the crowd. "People definitely knew who Garth Brooks was when they walked away," Norris said.[2]

One music industry manager described Brooks as "a cheerleader running around onstage, whipping up enthusiasm."[3] A reviewer described the reaction: "The audience hollers for him, feasts on him, lets itself go nuts with him."[4]

*Brooks performs with energy and raw emotion.*

And Brooks appreciated it. He remained connected to his fans. At one show that had been booked well before his album garnered hits, Brooks donated his entire proceeds to a charity benefiting cancer research. Though the fans may not have known about the generous gift, they saw a glimpse of that country gentleman at his concerts. After high-energy theatrics onstage, Brooks would quietly thank the crowd and ask if they would mind if he came back next year.[5]

That humbleness is part of the secret to his success. His manager Pam Lewis explained that "people can relate to him. He's chubby, he's balding, and sometimes his grammar's not the best. But he's very human."[6]

Meanwhile, the country music industry was taking off. Country radio stations were playing new songs by young artists such as Travis Tritt, Clint Black, Vince Gill, Pam Tillis, and Alan Jackson. Country music had suddenly become the second most popular music format. TNN: The Nashville Network had the fourth highest cable television viewer rating, even higher than MTV's. And sales of country music in 1990 totaled $660 million: 51 percent more than in 1989.[7]

What may be most surprising is that sales of country music were just as high in the Northeast as in the Midwest, with twice as many records sold in cities and suburbs as in rural areas.[8] People everywhere were now tuning in to country music.

Executives in the music business scrambled to figure out why. Some said that the controversial lyrics of rap and heavy metal were driving listeners away.

"Country is better to dance to . . . more sentimental [and] easier to listen to," explained one fan.[9] Other industry executives saw a link to the poor economy. The United States was in a recession during the early 1990s. "Whenever times get bad," said Steve Berger, president of a radio group with fourteen stations, "people return to their roots."[10]

Brooks summed up the mysterious increase in popularity. "We [were] a victim of good timing," he said. "I don't know what happened, I'm just glad it happened to us."[11]

That "aw-shucks" attitude is genuine. In October 1990, Garth Brooks was inducted into the Grand Ole Opry, something he considered his greatest professional achievement. "They gave me membership in a family . . . that includes . . . Mr. [Roy] Acuff and Ms. [Minnie] Pearl," Brooks said. "When someone asks to take a picture of me with [them] I'll . . . smile, but inside [I'm] thinking, 'I can't believe I'm doing this.'"[12]

Later that month, Brooks received two awards at the Country Music Awards—the CMA for his video "The Dance" and the Horizon Award. When his name was called, he brought Sandy along with him onstage.

In January 1991, "Unanswered Prayers," another single from the *No Fences* album, hit number one. Brooks had written the song based on his own experience of running into an old high school girlfriend years later. "The realization that what you have is the best for you . . . sure makes you sleep well at night," he said.[13] Another single, "Two of a Kind, Workin' on a Full House," was released as well.

Though Brooks often wrote about personal emotions, he was also interested in political issues. Across the globe, Saddam Hussein had invaded Kuwait. Multinational troops then bombarded military targets in Iraq with laser-guided bombs and cruise missiles. Brooks was not in the army, but he wanted to do his part to help the cause. Many singers joined together to create a music video, "Voices That Care." Their effort raised money for the Red Cross to help victims of the war. Garth Brooks lent his voice, alongside many other celebrities, including Celine Dion, Will Smith, and Whoopi Goldberg. During his own concerts, Brooks came on stage waving the red, white, and blue American flag. The patriotic crowds cheered. One such concert was in Norfolk, Virginia, where Garth performed free for the families of soldiers on active duty in the Persian Gulf.

Brooks's acts of charity were not limited to war efforts. Back in Nashville, he joined a large group of country singers and local children in recording "Let's Open Up Our Hearts" for a campaign encouraging kids to stay in school.

While Garth Brooks fever was spreading throughout the nation, Garth and Sandy returned to Yukon, Oklahoma, for a smaller tribute that meant much to the humble star. "Home of Garth Brooks" was painted on the city's water tower in honor of his contribution to country music. The fantasy he had enjoyed in his dreams of becoming a Nashville star had come true.

Though he did have a busy life as a performer,

when Garth was not on the road, he and Sandy spent time together much like any other young couple. They bought a home on eight acres just outside Nashville and began renovating it. While construction crews worked on the house, the two lived in a trailer on the hilltop property. When Garth and Sandy could finally move in, they took their time in choosing the right furniture. "We have no dining room table," Sandy said, without seeming to mind. "We can dance under the chandelier."[14]

These private times were rare, though, for Garth Brooks was in high demand. One night in April, rather than dancing in the dining room, the couple dressed in their best to attend the Academy of Country Music Awards. They sat in their seats, remembering the year before, when Garth did not win in any of the three categories he had been nominated for. This year, he had been nominated in seven categories.

Brooks did not remain seated long. He won six trophies. Brooks kept returning to the stage to accept another award: Best Male Vocalist, Best Video and Best Song for "The Dance," Best Single for "Friends in Low Places," Best Album for *No Fences,* and even the coveted Entertainer of the Year. Soon after, the country album *No Fences* hit number four on the pop charts. When the president of Capitol Records was told that *No Fences* had already reached sales of four million, he replied, "We got us a gusher here."[15]

Brooks was not about to merely sit back and enjoy the ride. He was always experimenting, pushing the boundaries. In his next project, would he push too far?

# The Thunder Rolls

A rumble of thunder rolls from the speakers. A patter of rain mingles with the strumming of a guitar. The first song on *No Fences,* "The Thunder Rolls," is an emotional one: A wife confronts her cheating husband. The lyrics in the song are dramatic enough, but Brooks again chose to add more depth to the story when making the music video. "I refuse to do a video that is just ordinary," he said. "It wastes the viewer's time and mine and the label's money."[1] In the video story, the cheating husband, played by Brooks in disguise, is also a wife abuser. The man returns home from an affair to a wife whose face is badly bruised. When she confronts him, a violent fight breaks out, ending with her pulling out a gun and shooting him.

The two country music channels, TNN and CMT, had been looking forward to the new Garth Brooks video. In early May 1991, they aired it for a few days, then suddenly stopped. The controversy was too strong. "The depiction of domestic violence is excessive and without an acceptable resolution," was TNN's explanation.[2] Bob Baker, the director of operations at CMT said, "We are an entertainment medium. . . . We are not about domestic violence, adultery and murder."[3]

Brooks was surprised and defended his decision to take on such a topic. "I would have never done something [the networks] couldn't use, but I'm not going to change what I do to fit their standards," he said. "They want to see the good side of real life . . . turn their backs on the bad."[4]

The fact that Brooks was willing to speak out on this topic showed he was both insightful and courageous. Though the taboo subject was unsettling to some, only a few years later country music singer Martina McBride would put out a video also illustrating the violence of spousal abuse, "Independence Day." Her video was played on television. "I'll take pride in thinking that 'The Thunder Rolls' had something to do with that," Brooks said.[5]

In July 1991, a tape of three Garth Brooks videos was put together for sale. Included were his signature songs "The Dance," the tender "If Tomorrow Never Comes," and brazenly, "The Thunder Rolls." Fans could view the controversial videotape and decide for themselves whether or not it was appropriate. In no time, they gave their answer. The tape hit number one on the Top Music Videos chart.

Later that month, Brooks performed a benefit concert with other bands, including Vince Gill, to raise money for farmers in trouble. All that summer, Brooks and his band continued touring. Trisha Yearwood, a friend from the old days in Nashville when they had been trying to break into the business, was the opening act. Her first album had just gone gold. Brooks and Yearwood now played large arenas instead of small clubs. Still, Brooks insisted on keeping ticket prices down. To see Garth Brooks perform in concert, a fan needed to spend only about $15 for a ticket, about half of what other top acts charged. "I believe in the Wal-Mart school of business," Brooks explained. "The less people pay for a product . . . the happier they are with it."[6]

It was not only low ticket prices that attracted people to his concerts. Word had spread of the great show Garth Brooks put on. Fans might see him smashing a guitar, running through a circle of flames and jumping into the crowd, or standing motionless with tears streaming down his face while singing a love song, holding a single rose in his hand. "[At] a Garth Brooks concert," explained a reporter for *Metro Source News,* "you will have two or three hours of the widest emotional range you can possibly have."[7]

People attended concerts in record numbers, and they also flocked to bars and dance halls to learn the new rage—line dancing. Many clubs advertised free dance lessons in the early evening, drawing crowds who would then stay all night to show off their new dance steps. Dance floors no longer held a mere scattering of couples locked in romantic embrace but were now flooded with people kicking up their heels, whirling and clapping together—and having a great time.

Brooks's busy schedule did not allow much time for songwriting. For his next album, he turned to other songwriters for some of the new material. During his search, he fell in love with a song, "Miss Rodeo," that he felt would be perfect for his friend Trisha Yearwood to record. But she disagreed. It did not bring out the same emotions in her as it did in him. "If you love this song so much, why don't you think about doing it?" Yearwood asked.[8]

*The popularity of country music sparked a new rage at dance clubs—line dancing.*

That is exactly what he did. "Rodeo" was the first single released from Garth Brooks's third album, *Ropin' the Wind.* Other songs on the album are Brooks's rendition of Billy Joel's "Shameless," a song that he had been performing in concert, and a ballad he had cowritten with Pat Alger, "What She's Doin' Now." Brooks had cowritten a song with Kim Williams about jealousy and revenge, like "The Thunder Rolls," but this time a touch of humor was added to the scenario, in "Papa Loved Mama."

Would the radio stations play it? They did.

Retailers could not wait to stock the album on their shelves, bringing the advance orders to more than a million copies. The retailers were not wrong. Fans bought up the CD as quickly as the stores could stock it. The CD went straight to number one on *both* country and pop charts.

Critics liked the album too. They did not mind that the songs on *Ropin' the Wind* were a mix of bluegrass, such as "Against the Grain," Western swing, as in "We Bury the Hatchet," and even some rock influence, with "The River." One reviewer wrote, "His second album 'No Fences' . . . went a long way toward making [Brooks] stand out. But it is this third album that tells the tale." She rated the performance as "his best yet."[9]

Garth Brooks was not the only entertainer changing what was on the country charts and crossing over into mainstream pop music. Greg Martin of the Kentucky Headhunters complained, "Some stations wouldn't play ["Walk Softly"] 'cause it was too heavy for country radio—someone even compared the guitar intro to Van Halen!"[10]

The music industry was changing, and not everyone was happy about it. One reviewer was just as surprised and annoyed as Lars Ulrich of the heavy metal band Metallica who was seen on MTV asking, "Who . . . is Garth Brooks?"[11] The reviewer felt his voice was "capable enough, but undistinguished," and that the songwriting was "predictable honky-tonk hokum."[12]

The reviewer did not sound happy that country music was invading the pop charts, and many country music artists were just as concerned. Some of the older musicians complained that their music was no longer getting played on radio stations. The disc jockeys were opting for the new, younger stars. Some of the younger musicians complained as well, saying that country music had gone pop. This dissatisfaction with the new direction of country music is recorded by TNN on its website that chronicles the history of country music. "While the whole world may have gone country, let's hope the world doesn't wake up one day to find real country gone."[13] Brooks worried about the change in country music as well. "That is the one thing that kills me," he said. "I woke up one day, and I never heard another George Jones or Merle Haggard tune on the radio."[14]

He hesitated to assign blame, though. Once the labels are gone, he said, music is music. "People are listening to what feels good to listen to, no matter what category that music falls under," he said.[15]

Fellow country singer Steve Wariner agreed, saying, "[Brooks] has really taken country to places it's never been before and exposed it to people that would not

*Holding a single rose in his hand, Brooks could sing a love song that brought the audience—and the singer himself—to tears.*

normally be accepting of it."[16] Brooks performed Billy Joel's pop song "Shameless" at the televised CMA Awards, using the opportunity to show America a different face of country music.

At the CMA Awards, "The Thunder Rolls" won Video of the Year, "Friends in Low Places" won Single of the Year, and *No Fences* brought in Album of the Year. But that was not all. The coveted Entertainer of the Year, honoring an artist who has shown excellence in the field of country music, was awarded to a tearful Garth Brooks. He was the first artist ever to win the Horizon Award as a newcomer one year and the Entertainer Award the following year.

President George H. W. Bush and First Lady Barbara Bush attended the awards ceremony. A longtime fan of country music, President Bush said, "Country music gives us a window on the real world." As he looked over the audience that filled the seats in the historic Grand Ole Opry House, he added, "It's easy to see why America loves country music, country music loves America."[17]

Two weeks later, the president proclaimed October 1991 as Country Music Month, offering his own explanation of the genre's popularity. "To listen to a country and western song is to hear the story of America set to music," he said. "Whether they tap their toes to the lively sound of bluegrass and honky-tonk or hum along with the rhythm and blues, country music lovers share an appreciation of the simple and most important things in life: faith, family, and friendship."[18]

In November, the Garth Brooks/Trisha Yearwood

duet "Like We Never Had a Broken Heart" hit the charts. In December, Brooks picked up another five awards at the *Billboard* Music Awards show, and he was included in the "25 Most Intriguing People of 1991" in *People* magazine. Even with his career at an all-time high, he managed to keep his personal life on track as well. By the end of the year, Garth and Sandy had announced they were to have their first child. "Whether it's passion or mowin' the lawn, he puts his heart and soul into all of it," Sandy said of her husband.[19]

How long could he keep up the pace?

# Breaking Records

$A$fter a whirlwind year of traveling, Garth and Sandy Brooks began 1992 at home on their twenty acres outside Nashville. Of course, even at home a superstar's public life asserts its presence. One night, they turned on the television to watch a compilation of Garth's concerts, broadcast as the NBC special "This Is Garth Brooks." In between taped performances there were clips of Brooks relaxing on a couch in an Oklahoma State jersey while band members and friends told stories about their pal, the celebrity. Sandy once admitted that if she had known the megastar her husband would one day become, she may not have married him. "I thought I was marrying the boy next door," she said.[1]

This Is Garth Brooks, *an hourlong television special, aired on NBC in January 1992.*

Over the years, though, Sandy Brooks would often accompany her husband in his other life—that of a celebrity. But during a flight to Los Angeles for the American Music Awards, she knew something was wrong. As soon as they landed at the airport, she was rushed to a hospital, fearing that her pregnancy was in danger. The doctors recommended that she keep off her feet for the next couple of months. They returned home to rest, and Garth took a break from work to spend time with his wife. "Business always came before family," he said. "But with a kid coming . . . life has to be slower."[2]

But how much slower? When a singing career takes off, there is not much time left for a personal life. Brooks suddenly realized that even if he wanted to, it would be impossible to quit. There were signed contracts for television appearances and product endorsements, and he had even started a shirt company. Now that the ball was rolling, he could not stop it.

Brooks would show up for an appearance, then realize he really did not want to be there. "I stayed up nights, wondering what I was going to do," he said.[3]

It was time to set priorities. "The one face I kept seeing in my mind was Sandy's," Brooks said. "Years are one thing you can't buy back."[4] He wrote down all that had been causing him anxiety, and started crossing things off that list. Next, it was time for negotiations. Brooks insisted on canceling some of his television commitments and cutting back on whatever he could. He negotiated more time to work on his next CD, insisting that he needed to be mentally happy in order to be able to produce quality music.

With deals finalized, Brooks could finally relax and look forward to the arrival of a new family member. When asked if her husband would help with the delivery, Sandy laughed. "The sight of blood and that man's gone," she said.[5]

By April, the doctors told Sandy she could travel with her husband to the Academy of Country Music Awards. Again, they set out for Los Angeles, where Garth picked up the Male Vocalist and Entertainer of the Year awards.

Little did the many country music celebrities know that while they were dressed in their glittering best, celebrating their successes and those of their peers, there was an entirely different scene out on the streets of Los Angeles. A controversial case had been tried in the courts, involving the beating of a black man, Rodney King, by four white police officers. The beating had been captured on videotape by a concerned citizen. That April afternoon, an all-white jury had announced its verdict. One officer was found guilty of using excessive force, but the others were cleared of any wrongdoing.

Word of this surprising verdict quickly spread. "The world saw the videotape [of the beating] and if that conduct is sanctioned by law in California, then we have to re-write the law," said California state senator Ed Smith.[6]

The senator was not the only one outraged by the jury's decision. People on the streets went wild. By late afternoon, many riots broke out. "Things are totally out of control here," said one Los Angeles police officer, " . . . and we expect it to get worse when it gets dark. . . . I hope we all live to see tomorrow."[7]

After the awards show, Garth and Sandy Brooks traveled back to Nashville. They were among the thousands of Americans who were horrified as they watched the television news reports documenting the violent riots that lasted three days. Garth had his own vehicle for expressing his emotions—songwriting. Within a few days of the riots, he had written "We Shall Be Free."

After a much-needed break from touring, Garth Brooks was ready to get back to work. "When I'm in between those speakers and the lights are up and the music is loud . . . I never want to get off the stage," he said.[8] He had been tired and had been worried about his wife, but now that he felt well rested and assured that Sandy's health and pregnancy were fine, it was time to return to his other life.

He opened his 1992 concert tour on June 2 in Denver, Colorado. The event would help raise money for an important cause, Feed the Children. Fans arrived at arenas with tickets in one hand and bags of food in the other. While Brooks performed onstage, trucks delivered the collected food to local agencies that would then distribute it to the needy in their areas.

It was around this time that Garth began referring to himself in the third person. He did not feel comfortable talking about his successes. It made him feel

*Colleen Brooks, Garth's mother, helped answer phones for the Feed the Children charity.*

as if he were a conceited superstar rather than the down-to-earth person he felt he truly was. "*Garth* is supposedly the biggest-selling solo act in the United States. I can't say *I* am," he explained. "That feels egotistical to me, and I hate that feeling."[9] But those successes were undeniable, so Brooks preferred to refer to his celebrity status as a separate person. In his concert tour program he explained, "There's GB the artist and Garth the lazy guy just hanging around the house."[10]

That everyday Garth probably is not lazy very often. In fact, during his tours, he is often seen working right along with the guys who unload and set up equipment. "He wasn't raised to sit and watch other people do things that he could do himself," said his road manager Mickey Weber, while admitting there are differences between the "two people."[11] "When [he is signing] autographs for nine hours . . . it's Garth working for 'Garth Brooks'."[12]

Even in the middle of a concert tour, Brooks managed to get home before Sandy gave birth. He was by her side in the delivery room, despite the sight of blood. "Being there when that child's first breath was taken . . . I was pumped," he said. "I [wandered] down the hall wanting to know if anybody else was going into delivery. I was ready!"[13] The cause of all this excitement? A baby girl was born July 8, 1992, named Taylor Mayne Pearl Brooks, after Grand Ole Opry star Minnie Pearl.

Only two months later, Garth Brooks was back on the charts. His fourth album, *The Chase,* shot to number one in just one week. It was full of songs that described feelings everyone can relate to: "That Summer," which Sandy helped write, about a lover's desire; "Learning to Live Again"; and "Somewhere Other Than the Night," which Garth performed at the CMA Awards where *Ropin' the Wind* won Album of the Year and he received yet another Entertainer of the Year award.

The song he had written after the Los Angeles riots, "We Shall Be Free," was included on the CD, but it met opposition from radio stations. One line in the song implied a defense of gay rights. "It was meant to be the truth as I saw it," Brooks said.[14] "I [had meant] relationships between all kinds of people—interracial [or] people with [different] forms of religion," he said. "But all the reviews focused in on *gay*."[15]

Perhaps that attention was due to the media's discovery that Garth's sister Betsy is gay. "The longer you live with it, the more you realize that it's just another form of people loving one another," Brooks said.[16]

In the fall, Brooks released a holiday album, *Beyond the Season,* a combination of traditional Christmas carols and original material. He donated one dollar from the sale of each CD to Feed the Children, raising more than $2 million.

By the end of the year, it was obvious that Garth Brooks had become a megastar. He was not just a popular entertainer to country music fans. He was the leader of a trend where people of all ages all over America were tuning in to country music stations. *Ropin' the Wind* had sold more than any other album in *any category* that year, with *No Fences* following close behind.

Garth's father worried about how his son would be able to handle all the success. On visits, he would pull his son aside to ask, "You know you're not living in the real world, don't you?"[17] Garth does know. It helps to have his family and old friends around him. They have known the real Garth Brooks and are able to separate him from Garth the celebrity. They help keep his ego in check. In an interview, Brooks described what his normal day might be like. He might be woken up in the afternoon by a childhood friend, now his manager, who gives him his schedule for the week. Then his brother comes along to discuss financial details. Later, Garth goes onstage, joining band members that include his sister and an old college roommate.

While performing for huge audiences, Brooks remains true to his values. Millions watched him sing the National Anthem at the 1993 Super Bowl, not knowing that he had insisted that patriotic clips from his "We Shall Be Free" video be aired as he sang.

*By writing songs, Brooks could express his emotions about political events as well as personal ones.*

He played two concerts at the Great Western Forum in Los Angeles, raising a million dollars to help rebuild sections of the city that had been devastated during the riots.

Garth Brooks had already broken many CD sales records and had won countless awards. That summer, Brooks broke yet another record. A concert was to be held in September in Texas Stadium with sixty-five thousand seats. The show sold out in an hour and a half. Thousands of fans who had been waiting in line for days, yet still missed out on tickets, were not disappointed for long. A second show was announced, again selling out in about an hour and a half. Garth announced a third show, which took a whole two hours to sell out. Finally, a fourth show was added. Because Brooks would lip-synch to tapes of the previous concerts in order to film close-up shots, the sixty-five thousand tickets were free. Nowhere in the country had this ever happened before.

How could he possibly outdo himself again?

# A Night Like Tonight

Just after the beginning of his 1993 World Tour, Garth Brooks released his fifth album, *In Pieces.* Though one reviewer wrote, "Brooks has made one of his worst decisions by recording a misguided anthem titled 'American Honky-Tonk Bar Association,'" he did admit, "the rest of this album is . . . well conceived and executed, covering country, blues and full-out rock."[1] What the critic had not known was that "American Honky-Tonk Bar Association" would soon become a favorite sing-along song at concerts. Another reviewer said the new CD "proves again that today's country music is virtually anything Garth chooses to call country."[2] About the variety of songs, the critic continued, "The music's appeal [is that] it sings the detailed stories of its listeners' lives."[3] In "Standing Outside the Fire," Brooks advises taking risks, while in "Ain't Going Down ('Til the Sun Comes Up)" he describes young kids doing just that.

In the fall, Brooks took his tour to Canada. Tickets for shows in each of the six cities were sold out in less than two hours. In Edmonton, seventeen thousand seats in Northlands Coliseum were snapped up in a record-breaking forty-five minutes. Brooks was surprised that his popularity had spread so far. "I went from wondering if anybody would recognize my name to being in the middle of a show," he said, "throwing a guitar high . . . and letting it smash."[4]

Sandy and Taylor, now a toddler, were with Brooks in Canada. The young family was expecting a second child. It seemed Garth was doing his best to keep his professional career and personal life on an even balance. "I want my musical life," he explained, "[but when] I step off that stage I want that family life."[5]

For a person with wealth and fame, keeping those two lives separate can be difficult. It would be easy to get caught up in a different lifestyle, but Brooks has managed to remain down-to-earth. "I try and stay away from limousines," he said. "It's not my way."[6] Instead, as he told an appreciative crowd after a performance in North Carolina, "The real rewards I'm looking for are nights like tonight."[7]

Other nights that must have offered that same sense of personal reward were the shows in Texas

Stadium. They had one of the biggest productions ever, with new special effects to please the 65,000 fans, many of whom had camped in line for days waiting to buy tickets. The lights went down and the crowd yelled its approval. Suddenly, a man in jeans and cowboy hat appeared from beneath the stage in a cloud of smoke, yelling, "Hellooo, Texas!" As he performed "Standing Outside the Fire," Garth walked through flames surrounding the stage. As he sang "The Thunder Rolls," flashes of lightning, sounds of rumbling thunder, and even a misty rain filled the stadium. Later, he took the stage alone, strumming a few chords on his acoustic guitar. The audience joined him in singing "Unanswered Prayers."

The tender feeling would change yet again when the band returned on stage to rock the crowd with "Ain't Going Down ('Til the Sun Comes Up)." As Garth belted out the lyrics, he suddenly flew high into the air and all around the stadium. With the wire that held him barely visible, Garth flew up to the fans in the furthest seats, giving everyone in the stadium a close view of the crazy superstar.

A top music industry consultant, Andy Francis, said he had never seen anything like a Garth Brooks show: "I've seen Prince, Springsteen, and Bowie, but Garth controls the audience like no one I've ever seen. He had the whole place in the palm of his hand."[8]

Brooks may have outperformed some popular acts, but he still remained true to his own musical heroes. In November, Garth sang Billy Joel's "New York State of Mind" to a crowd on Long Island. Later,

*What a show! Brooks flew through the air during this performance.*

he met members of one of his old favorite rock bands, KISS, after one of his shows. They had read that Brooks mentioned them as being influential to him as a teenager. "I see [the influence]. I see it in your show," said KISS member Paul Stanley. "I'm flattered."[9] Brooks was just as flattered. He later recorded "Hard Luck Woman" for a KISS tribute album, with KISS playing backup. That was as far as the musical relationship went, for Brooks said if the band who appeared in painted faces had wanted him to join them onstage, he would "have to think what my face would look like painted . . . maybe a big wagon wheel."[10]

During the 1993 holiday season, Brooks had a chance to show the true spirit of giving. He spotted a young couple carrying a one-year-old daughter and bags of groceries and offered them a ride home. They told the stranger they were walking because their car had broken down and they could not afford the repairs. An hour later, Brooks returned to their home and handed the surprised couple the keys to a 1986 Chevrolet Caprice Classic. The woman asked if he was Garth Brooks, but the generous "Santa" only smiled and said he was a big fan.[11]

To begin the European part of the worldwide tour in 1994, Brooks invited Susan Ashton to open for him. She had previously sung background vocals for some of his songs. "I got a videotape of his Texas Stadium shows in Dallas and I freaked out!" she said. Luckily, Brooks gave her plenty of support. "He encouraged me and helped me move forward as a performer."[12] After some successful shows in Ireland, Brooks returned home to the United States, but it was not for the Academy of Country Music Awards. Minutes before being named Entertainer of the Year and winning Best Video for "We Shall Be Free," daughter August Anna arrived to join the Brooks family. "If Garth Brooks thinks being with his wife when she's having a baby is more important than [this trophy]," comedian Jay Leno joked, "I don't know where his values are."[13]

Not everyone agreed with the CMA judges' admiration of Brooks as a country music singer. One person who disagreed was a television writer and producer who preferred the George Jones or Gram Parsons style of country music. "[Garth Brooks] is country music for people who hate country music," he complained in *Gentlemen's Quarterly.*[14]

Fortunately for Brooks, his critics were in the minority, not only in the United States but all around the world. After rehearsing through the spring and summer, Brooks was ready for a world tour, beginning in New Zealand. From there, Brooks entertained audiences in Australia, Spain, Germany, and France. Some experiences in the different countries were eye-opening. After seeing African-American Vicki Hampton, one of Brooks's backup singers, a concert-goer in France said, "[He] couldn't understand how country music could have a black person in it 'cause . . . that's what country music was against."

Brooks responded, "When you hear that, man, your skin just crawls . . . until you realize that's what you're out there for—to educate people on that stuff."[15]

Of course, what that French person did not know was that there has been African-American influence in country music. Many African Americans in the rural South played the banjo, fiddle, or harmonica in a style that contributed to country music's early development. "While it is a stretch to say that black people gave the world country music, African immigrants and their descendants did give America's heartland music a range of musical style influences," wrote Pamela Foster, author of a book on the African-American influence in country music.[16]

Still, that French man at the Garth Brooks concert was not completely wrong. Except for Charley Pride, there have not been many black artists who sustained a career in country music. "Country music, with its profound debt to African-American musical traditions, has become so deeply associated with whites that black artists seem wildly out of place when they perform it," wrote one journalist.[17]

By traveling to different countries, Brooks was being educated, too. "I see that the people in Dallas [Texas] react the same as the people in Dublin [Ireland], who react the same as the people in Ottawa [Canada]," Brooks said. "My faith in the fact that we're all an awful lot alike just gets stronger every day."[18]

The only concert in the United States that year was a benefit in Los Angeles for One Voice, an organization that helps low-income families. Yet, even in his absence, the American fans did not forget him. In the fall of 1994, *The Garth Brooks Collection: Garth's Favorites* was sold at McDonald's restaurants. Though it was not a hit reported by *Billboard,* which tracks only the sales at retail stores, it could still be considered the best-selling album in the country. Boyz II Men's "II" was number one according to *Billboard,* at one million copies, but *The Garth Brooks Collection* had sold more than three million copies during that same time frame.[19] One dollar from each "Collection" CD purchase was donated to Ronald McDonald House, an organization that houses families near hospitals in which their children are being treated for serious illness.

By the end of the year, Garth Brooks was celebrating 11 million in sales for *No Fences,* 10 million for *Ropin' the Wind,* and a successful new compilation release with the songs that had made him famous, *Garth Brooks/The Hits.* When he accepted the award for Favorite Male Country Artist at the American Music Awards show, he told the audience how much he missed them. He had been performing overseas for almost a year, and still had almost another year left on the tour.

Brooks spent much of 1995 on tour, with his family at his side. When able, Brooks returned to the four-hundred-acre farm he calls "Some Day Valley." "It's where my girls go and watch the deer at sunset," Brooks said, "and it's where we go to fight and laugh and wrestle."[20] It's where the superstar can spend hours among the hay and apple trees, staying in touch with reality. He can do chores, like driving his tractor and taking the garbage out on trash collection day. Even trick-or-treating with the kids was special to him. During a Halloween fest he dressed up as Mickey Mouse, a costume that concealed his true identity. "It was so much fun to be out with people and everybody treated [me] the same," he said.[21]

When he was not performing, Brooks was busy writing new material. But after spending afternoons with Sandy and helping her tend to the little ones, Taylor and August, the writing was often slow going. "By the time they go to bed, I'm worn out, so I don't stay up 'til 4 a.m. writing like I used to," he said.[22]

Still, he managed to write some new songs. The results were, among others, "She's Every Woman," cowritten with Victoria Shaw, and "It's Midnight Cinderella," written with Kim Williams and Kent Blazy. "Ireland," cowritten with Stephanie Davis and Jenny Yates, was a tribute to the country he had enjoyed touring in. "[It's] like a postcard that thanks them," said Brooks.[23] He revised "The Fever" in a way that, one reviewer wrote, "transforms the Aerosmith rock hit into a heart-thumping fiddle-laced rodeo song."[24] "The Beaches of Cheyenne," written with Dan Roberts and Bryan Kennedy, was meant to be a song "that would marry George Strait and Jimmy Buffett," said Brooks, but once they got started, they realized, "it was not going to be a funny song."[25] Instead, it turned out to be a legendary tale of a woman mourning her dead lover, unable to take back mean words she had said the last time she saw him. These songs made up *Fresh Horses.* When released, the compilation CD sold 480,000 copies in one week.

Another song on the CD, "The Change," had a special meaning for Garth. Back in April, he and the rest of a stunned nation watched news reports of a terrorist attack in downtown Oklahoma City, near Brooks's own hometown. A bomb inside a rental truck had exploded, destroying half of the Murrah Federal Building. After the smoke had cleared and the rubble was searched, it was determined that 168 people had lost their lives in the bombing. Three weeks later, Brooks heard a song that offered hope that people will continue to do good in a world where such horrors could exist and decided he had to record it. When filming a music video of the song, Brooks used actual news footage from the terrible disaster.

The premiere of "The Change" video was during the American Music Awards show. "[It was] very powerful," said country singer Ronnie Dunn. "I couldn't even look, I just looked down."[26] He was not the only one in the audience affected. Many viewers were seen wiping tears from their eyes.

That was not the only surprise Brooks would offer during that awards show. Neil Diamond walked onstage to present the last award for Favorite Artist of the Year. The nominees were Green Day, TLC, Boys II Men, Hootie and the Blowfish, and Garth Brooks. Diamond peeled off the seal, opened the envelope and announced the winner: "Garth Brooks."

Brooks slowly walked to the stage. "I just kept saying to myself, 'Man, I don't deserve this,'" he later explained.[27] After taking off his hat and bowing in acceptance, he set the trophy on the podium. He told the surprised audience that he could not accept the award because he did not believe in the concept of choosing one artist out of so many different types of music. "I'm going to leave [the trophy] here," he said, then walked away.[28]

The giant superstar had shown his humble side to the world. What side of Garth Brooks would be revealed next?

# A Charitable Heart

In March 1996, Brooks was about to travel again, this time for a three-year worldwide tour, scheduled to kick off in Atlanta, Georgia. Though *Fresh Horses* had sold more than two and a half million copies, it was considered only moderately successful compared to the $725 million in sales of Garth Brooks music during the previous seven years. He hoped the new tour would provide the spark needed to ignite his career again. "If the record and ticket sales don't tell me that I'm stirring things up or changing people's lives, then I think it's time for me to hang it up," Brooks said in an interview.[1]

Again Brooks insisted on keeping ticket prices low. While many top acts were charging more than $60 a ticket, Brooks kept his ticket price under $20. He wanted the fans to leave his concerts feeling their money had been well spent. "We're all making a great living, the band and the crew, but we're not out to book a vacation in Hawaii with each ticket sold," he said.[2]

The tour would again be a family affair. Sandy, now pregnant with their third child, followed along with Taylor and August in her own vehicle, which they called the Girls' Bus. During the lengthy periods of time traveling between shows, Garth read and responded to his fan mail. When a sixteen-year-old girl asked for advice on how she could reach her own goals, Brooks told her to finish school before anything else. "The more education we have, the less fighting we're gonna do," he said. "The more we talk things over, the less often we'll reach for a weapon. Education is everything."[3]

Brooks was able to connect with fans personally even when performing in front of huge audiences. At one concert in Cleveland, Ohio, Brooks walked to the edge of the stage to ask a nine-year-old boy how he knew all the words to the song he had just played. To the amusement of the audience, the boy answered that he had seen Garth Brooks on television with the Muppets. Brooks looked around the stage for a souvenir the boy could take home, then took off his guitar and announced, "This'll do." Loud screams of approval burst forth from the audience as Brooks autographed the instrument and handed it to the surprised boy.[4]

*Talented, funny, enthusiastic, humble, charitable—Brooks has revealed many facets of his personality and character.*

In July, the Garth Brooks tour had reached Denver, Colorado. One fan, Coral Volland, was astonished when two crew members took her from her seat and brought her backstage. She was given cameras, flowers, and other souvenirs, along with a wheelbarrow to hold the merchandise. That was not all. There was Garth Brooks, holding a set of keys to a new Chevrolet Z-28 Camaro! The reason? It was impossible to thank all his fans personally, so she had been chosen as a representative because she had purchased the one millionth ticket for the tour.[5] "When Garth does these crazy things, he makes people feel connected to him," said one reporter. "People feel like Garth cares about them."[6] But Brooks denied that his actions were so crazy. "Everything I have . . . is due to the people who buy CDs or come out to concerts," he said. "It's those people who have made my career possible."[7]

There was one place for fun that Brooks did not want to miss—Fan Fair. This year, Brooks was not scheduled to attend, but when he drove up in his truck and walked in, fans quickly recognized and surrounded him. Did he mind the attention? He did not seem to, for he stood there talking with fans, shaking their hands and signing autographs—for twenty-three hours straight! When asked if he was afraid when surrounded by all those strangers, he merely answered, "In the middle of those people is when I feel the safest."[8]

Soon after, on July 28, 1996, daughter number three, Allie Colleen Brooks, was born. The bus that Sandy, Taylor, and August had been traveling in with their nanny and teacher could still be called the Girls' Bus.

In October, the tour had traveled to New Brunswick, Canada. A five-year-old boy who had been diagnosed with brain cancer eagerly awaited his idol's arrival. With help from Children's Wish Foundation, the boy met his favorite singer, who came armed with posters, tapes, pictures and T-shirts. But Garth did not stop there. He brought the boy onstage to enjoy a few songs, then introduced him to the audience. The boy could always cherish those memories. Even better, his mother later reported that her son's health was improving.[9]

*Brooks connected with his fans—and often surprised them, too. He gave this young cancer patient a guitar during a concert.*

Later that month, Sandy and Garth celebrated their tenth wedding anniversary by renewing their marriage vows. The years together had not always been easy. Garth told Sandy, "Being married to an entertainer is like dog years: For every year of marriage, it must feel like seven."[10]

In February 1997, Melinda and Ricky Huffman were seated at the very back of the Charleston Coliseum, waiting for the Garth Brooks concert to begin. They were surprised when crew members came to their seats and asked them to come backstage. There was Garth Brooks, laden with gifts, including a 1997 Chevrolet Tahoe and a trip to the islands (they could choose between the U.S. Virgin Islands and the Cayman Islands). "You are our two millionth customer," he explained, happy that the two-millionth ticket sale came from this particular concert. "[They] waited [in line for tickets] in temperatures that were around three [degrees] below," he said.[11]

From there, the tour traveled back to Europe. The stage was designed to appear as if the band arrived via spaceship, without Garth. "The band prowled around the stage, heightening the already electric atmosphere by playing crescendos of music that made us all think that Garth was about to appear," described a concertgoer in Dublin, Ireland. "He had a catwalk running along in front of the stage, all 450 feet of it, and at times [Brooks] would run from one end to the other and back, but still have enough breath to sing when he got there."[12]

After the Ireland shows, Garth flew home to

Oklahoma to be with his mother, who was undergoing radiation treatment for throat cancer. She was very proud of her son. "Garth says he wants to bring prayer back to the dinner table and an American flag back to the front porch," she said. "I think that's wonderful."[13] The next couple of months, Brooks held marathon sessions in the recording studio that "kept him from thinking for long periods of time about his mom," said his road manager.[14]

Though he had raced to complete the album, because of some differences between Brooks and his record label, he decided not to release it at the free concert in New York's Central Park, which would be broadcast live on HBO. "Nobody wins if Brooks keeps it in house," said his producer Jimmy Bowen, "including him."[15] Brooks agreed. "When we decided not to put an album out, we walked away from six and one-half million orders," he said.[16] The record label executives may have felt Brooks was being stubborn, but he insisted on settling grievances with the company before releasing the album. "If the industry is going somewhere that Garth does not feel is right for Garth to go," Brooks said, "then Garth has to stand up and say, 'Guys, I can't make that trip with you.'"[17]

On August 7, 1997, Garth Brooks hit New York City. Some fans camped out overnight to ensure good seats, while others wandered in from work, wondering what the crowd of people in cowboy hats was doing in Central Park.

Not everyone enjoyed the show that brought country fans stampeding to the city. "[Anyone] can mock the Madonna-style telephone operator microphone that allowed him to run tirelessly across the stage like a checker-shirted ping-pong ball," wrote one critic.[18] But that opinion was surely overruled by the crowd, estimated at 250,000 strong. Though he was the first country singer to perform a major concert in Central Park, he did not do it alone. Billy Joel joined him onstage to perform "New York State of Mind," and Don McLean accompanied him for his classic "American Pie."

Though she did not join him onstage, Garth was proud to announce that his daughter Taylor sings too. Her first song was her dad's "Fever." "She knew one word and she'd run around naked in the house screaming 'Fever!'"[19]

Brooks chose a different female singer, Trisha Yearwood, to record a duet, "In Another's Eyes." They had become good friends back in Nashville before either of them had signed record deals, and had sung vocals on each other's albums through the years. Finally, they collaborated on a duet. Of Yearwood, Brooks said, "She could sing the yellow pages and make them sound good."[20] Yearwood shares the praise. "The music he creates is passionate and from the heart," she said. "Garth is also one of the most generous friends I know."[21] She surprised the crowd by appearing onstage at his concert in San Jose, California. Fans reacted with enthusiastic screams and applause. "I was truly overwhelmed by the crowd's response," she said. "Thank goodness Garth was there to hold me up or I surely would have fainted!"[22]

The following month, Brooks won Entertainer of the Year at the Country Music Association's awards show at the Grand Ole Opry House. He was not able to attend the show because he was busy performing in Lincoln, Nebraska. It was at one of the shows in Lincoln where Chad and Amy McClintock were brought backstage as the buyers of the three-millionth ticket of the tour. They were awarded a $9,000 shopping spree, a Chevrolet pickup truck, and a BMW convertible. "It's our way of saying thank you for . . . feeding our family," Brooks explained to the surprised couple.[23]

Though tickets for Garth Brooks's concerts were still bought up quickly, growth of the country music industry was finally slowing. Some industry executives felt it was because Brooks had not released an album since 1995. "Garth represents a larger portion of country sales than any single artist in the rock field," explained an executive from the Country Music Association.[24] Country singer Randy Travis had a different opinion. "We've gone from a hit album being 300,000 units, to when you sell 300,000 units you're dropped from the label," he complained. "We got away from traditional music again and started hitting more cross-over stuff. . . . The quality of songs has suffered."[25]

In November 1997, Brooks finally released his first album in almost two years. *Sevens* had originally been scheduled for release on the seventh day of the seventh month of 1997. Brooks appeared at Kmart store number 7777, located at 770 Broadway in New

York City, to perform some of the new songs, talk with fans, and answer questions.

"The album is plenty down home," wrote a critic, "with bits of western swing and sagebrush shuffle . . . the music has a lithe sophistication."[26] Fans must have agreed. In less than two months *Sevens* had sold 3.7 million copies. In February 1998, Brooks appeared on the television show *Oprah*, where he pledged to donate proceeds from the album to Oprah Winfrey's Angel Network of charities. On another show, *Live with Regis and Kathie Lee*, Brooks was interviewed. When the show went to commercial, Brooks was handed gifts from the audience, including a teddy bear and red rose from a woman at the back. With thirty seconds left in the commercial break, Brooks jumped up from his seat onstage to bound up the steps and give the woman a big hug. Though he raced back to his seat in time, Regis Philbin was the one who gave it all away. "You're not going to believe what just happened!" he told the television audience. "Can we get a shot of that woman?" The cameras panned to the back row where the woman stood smiling, and crying happy tears.[27]

While promoting this new album, Brooks was also busy with a few other projects. These were sure to amaze his fans, even those who were used to his surprises.

# New Faces

$A$ thirty-six year-old man in a dark blue number-seven jersey stood in the outfield of Peoria stadium, shagging fly balls and fielding grounders. He took his turn at home plate, swinging away at baseballs. He ran at full speed and slid hard. Who was this ballplayer? None other than Garth Brooks, fulfilling an old fantasy of playing professional baseball. "The slide felt good," he said. "But I'll feel it tomorrow."[1]

Though baseball is his favorite sport, Brooks was willing to give golf a try as well. A former classmate from Oklahoma State University persuaded him to play in the Pro Classic's pro-am scramble in Spokane, Washington. Fans laughed along with Brooks as he battled with his golf swing, often sending a slice into the woods. In between holes Brooks signed auto-graphs on hats, shirts, or scorecards. Once, after hitting a good piece of ground behind his golf ball, he signed the divot. "I wrote a whole song on it," Brooks teased. "It was big enough!"[2]

While Brooks took time out for sports, he still had time for his music. He recorded a Bob Dylan song, "To Make You Feel My Love," for the sound track for the movie *Hope Floats.* At first he was not crazy about the song, but while watching the film Brooks was caught up in the emotion. "When I'm sitting there watching it on the big screen, they stuck a recorder in front of me," he said. "[The song] is me and my guitar in that movie seat watching the film. The moment was there."[3]

Soon after, Brooks released *The Limited Series,* a boxed set of his first six CDs, and in the fall, *Garth Brooks: Double Live,* recordings from his live perfor-mances. "I kinda wanted to bring the ticket to life, the memory that you take," he said. "This was a way for people to . . . re-live that experience."[4] That they did. "[The fans] sing along through most of 'The Dance' and on 'Unanswered Prayers' they almost drown out Brooks," wrote one reviewer.[5] Another critic poked fun at Garth's unbelievable goal—to sell one million copies in one week. "And then he wants to shoot fire out of his eyes like a god," he joked.[6] Though unbelievable, the goal was not unattainable. *Garth Brooks: Double Live* achieved the best first-week sales of any album in American music history, selling 1,085,373 units in its first week. In an attempt to explain this, Tennessee governor Don Sundquist said, "Garth is an entertainer who touches people in a very personal way. . . . His enthusiasm and dedication . . . bring people together in a way that only heartfelt music can."[7]

By the end of 1998, Brooks had finished his world tour, appeared on *The Tonight Show with Jay Leno,* broadcast a closed-circuit performance to 2,400 Wal-Mart stores, and answered questions from fans on a live TV special. He needed time off. "I haven't got to spend hardly any time in the past six months with my children," he complained. "And I would love to *write* again."[8]

After a few months off, however, Brooks was itching to get busy again—this time creating a project dear to his heart. Garth used his love of baseball to form a foundation involving Major League Baseball and children, Touch 'em All: Teammates for Kids, in which players donate money in accordance with their game performance. Foundation president Bo Mitchell said, "Garth wanted to touch as many kids as possible. He wanted to touch them all. As soon as I said that, I knew we were on to something."[9] All the money raised on the ball field goes to the kids.

One of the first players to pledge a donation was Colorado Rockies player Larry Walker. He remembered a few years back when he had attended a Garth Brooks concert. He had given one of his jerseys to Brooks in exchange for tickets to the show. Halfway through the show, Garth took off his shirt and was wearing the jersey underneath. "It was one of the greatest moments of my life," Walker said.[10] Ken Griffey, Jr., signed up early as well, pledging $1,000 for each home run he hits. "I want it to give opportunities to kids that might not have it," Brooks said of the money raised. "Those kids go on to do something with their lives that changes the world for a better place."[11] Within a year, the foundation raised about $12 million in cash and gifts to donate to various causes, including a pediatric AIDS foundation and a school for the deaf.

Not only did he recruit ballplayers for his foundation, but Brooks tried living out his dream of playing the game with professional ballplayers. When San Diego Padres owner John Moores heard of Brooks's desire to play with the team, he admitted, "He's got an athletic build and a big pair of wheels."[12] Though the tryouts were tough, Brooks said, "Other than playing music for a living, it's the most fun thing I've done."[13] On the field, that excitement was clear. During a game against the Chicago White Sox, Garth smacked a line drive down the center. The pitcher tried for it, the second baseman dove for it, but Brooks ran hard. He made it to the base, safe, and immediately gave the Chicago first baseman a big hug. "I bet that base hit to him means more than if he sells another million records," said the Padres general manager.[14]

Seeing their favorite country music star having fun with professional baseball players may have seemed strange to some fans, but Brooks's next project was sure to surprise everyone much more. He recorded a new album of "hits" that were to be used as the soundtrack for a future movie, *The Lamb*. But he performed the songs as an invented character named Chris Gaines. Gaines was described as a pop-rocker from Australia who sings in a higher vocal range than the country Brooks. As Gaines, Brooks took off his cowboy hat, put on a wig, and donned makeup to give his face a pale, thin look.

"Garth will be taking gambles as long as he is an entertainer," said American entertainment icon Dick Clark.[15] Not only did Brooks gamble on the CD, but he also played the role of Gaines in a VH1 documentary, with real music artists being interviewed about their relationships with the fictional Gaines. "[The idea] allows him to do things that wouldn't fit his Garth Brooks persona or perhaps be accepted by Garth Brooks fans," said movie critic Roger Ebert.[16]

Unfortunately, that turned out to be a problem. Three months after the CD's release, only about half a million copies had sold. "Obviously Garth Brooks fans did not buy the Chris Gaines album," said one industry manager.[17] "[Some people think] I've actually changed my name and I'm going for this different kind of thing," said Brooks. "It's not that way at all. It's a character in a movie and this is his music."[18] Later, he acknowledged his fans may have understood, but still did not embrace the strange character. "I don't think people dug me playing someone so opposite of me," he said.[19]

Perhaps it was the lack of success as Chris Gaines, along with low sales of his holiday album,

*The Magic of Christmas,* that led Brooks to think of retirement once again. His personal life was taking a toll as well. His mother, who had always believed in him, lost her battle with cancer in August 1999. In addition, Garth and Sandy, who had quietly separated in March 1999, were struggling to repair their relationship. "What I need to do is work on my marriage . . . because it needs it," Brooks said.[20] During an interview on TNN's *Crook & Chase,* Brooks admitted, "Music is not the first thing in my life anymore."[21] He hinted that he might announce his retirement by the next year. Backstage at the American Music Awards, Brooks said of his marriage, "We're trying real hard."[22]

Unfortunately, whatever they tried was not enough. In an October 2000 interview in *Billboard,* Brooks announced that he and Sandy were ending their fourteen-year marriage. (Their divorce became final in December 2001.) Still, he remains focused on raising his daughters, who live with Sandy. "I want to try and become for them what my dad was and still is for me," Brooks said.[23]

In November 2000, at a gala event celebrating his record sales of 100 million albums, Brooks announced his retirement. He conceded that he was planning another album but would not tour again until his youngest daughter, four-year-old Allie, started college. "The stuff that I am pulling away from is the stuff that takes me away from home," Brooks said.[24]

Though his family may be his top priority, a man like Garth Brooks will find it hard to stay away from

*Brooks celebrated 100 million album sales at a private party in Nashville, Tennessee.*

something he has been so passionate about. He began with a dream and accomplished even more than he had thought possible. Not only has the country boy from Oklahoma achieved personal success, but he has broken many records in the music industry and has won every prize in the business. He can boast a Grammy, many CMA, ACM, and People's Choice awards, *Billboard* Music awards, albums that hit multiplatinum, and eighteen number-one hit singles, including two that certified diamond (ten million in sales). Ticket sales and concert attendance have been phenomenal. This kind of success is hard to walk away from.

Perhaps that is why so many friends who know Brooks find the retirement hard to believe. "He is bursting with talent, and he'll explode if he doesn't perform," said Michael Greene, chief executive of the National Academy of Recording Arts and Sciences.[25]

While he may stay away from touring for a while, Brooks does want to spend more time writing music. He will relax with friends and band members, creating new verses and trying different harmonies—returning

*Many fans find it hard to believe that Brooks will stay retired.*

to where he had begun his life as a musician, with dreams of the future.

"We shouldn't deny Garth the dreams we all have . . . to do something we haven't done before," said Dick Clark. "If you don't have that . . . there's something missing in your life."[26]

"He'll be back," a fan predicted during a Dixie Chicks concert. "And when he does [return], he'll be bigger than ever."[27]

In the meantime, fans can take comfort in the treasures Brooks has recorded over the years. He gives them all the credit for his success and thanks them for his life. "If it ended tonight," said an emotional Garth Brooks when he announced his retirement, "it is complete."[28]

Just a year later, in November 2001, Brooks was back with a new album. *Scarecrow* was promoted with three television specials on the CBS network. Still, the father of three insists that he will not do any concert tours while his daughters are young. Instead, soccer practices are the top priority for the self-described "dad who occasionally sings."[29] That occasional singing could call Brooks out of retirement for additional projects—perhaps an album with old friend Trisha Yearwood or another Chris Gaines pop music collection.[30] Garth Brooks fans can only wait to see what their beloved superstar will dream up next.

1962—Troyal Garth Brooks is born in Tulsa, Oklahoma, on February 7.

1980—Graduates from Yukon High School; enters Oklahoma State University.

1984—Graduates from Oklahoma State University.

1985—Moves to Nashville for country music career, but quickly returns home.

1986—Forms band Santa Fe; marries Sandy Mahl.

1987—Moves to Nashville.

1988—Signs with Capitol Records; forms touring band Stillwater.

1989—Debut album *Garth Brooks* is released and becomes best seller.

1990—Releases *No Fences;* inducted into the Grand Ole Opry.

1991—Wins six Academy of Country Music Awards; releases *Ropin' The Wind.*

1992—NBC television special *This Is Garth Brooks* airs; daughter Taylor Mayne Pearl is born; releases *The Chase.*

1993—Performs national anthem at Super Bowl; releases *In Pieces.*

1994—Daughter August Anna is born; releases *The Garth Brooks Collection;* begins World Tour; releases *The Hits.*

1995—Releases *Fresh Horses.*

1996—Daughter Allie Colleen is born.

1997—Performs in New York City's Central Park; releases *Sevens.*

1998—Releases *The Limited Series* and *Garth Brooks: Double Live.*

1999—Forms the foundation Touch 'em All: Teammates for Kids.

2000—Announces his retirement.

2001—Releases *Scarecrow,* which he promotes with three television specials.

# Discography

*Garth Brooks* (Capitol, 1989)

*No Fences* (Capitol, 1990)

*Ropin' the Wind* (Capitol, 1991)

*Beyond the Season* (Liberty, 1992)

*The Chase* (Liberty, 1992)

*In Pieces* (Liberty, 1993)

*The Garth Brooks Collection* (Pearl, 1994)

*The Hits* (Liberty, 1994)

*Fresh Horses* (Capitol, 1995)

*Sevens* (Capitol, 1997)

*The Limited Series* (Capitol, 1998)

*Double Live* (Capitol, 1998)

*In the Life of Chris Gaines* (Capitol, 1999)

*The Magic of Christmas* (Capitol, 1999)

*Scarecrow* (Capitol, 2001)

## Chapter 1.  Standing Outside the Fire

1. Karen Schoemer, "The World According to Garth," *Newsweek,* March 16, 1998, p. 70.

2. Jane Sanderson, "For Garth Brooks, Country Music's Newest Nova, Nashville Proves Sweeter the Second Time Around," *People Weekly,* September 3, 1990, p. 91.

3. Anthony DeCurtis, "Ropin' the Wind: Garth Brooks, the Rolling Stone Interview," *Rolling Stone,* April 1, 1993, p. 34.

4. Ibid.

5. Ibid.

6. Ibid., p. 35.

7. Jo Sgammato, *American Thunder: The Garth Brooks Story* (New York: Ballantine Books, 1999), p. 21.

8. Sanderson, p. 92.

9. Jay Cocks, "Country Classicists," *Time,* September 24, 1990, p. 92.

10. Gerry Wood and Larry Holden, "Garth Rewrites History of Country Music," *Country Weekly,* March 23, 1999, <http://www.countryweekly.com/archives/3_23_99/brooks.htm> (September 1, 1999).

11. Ibid.

## Chapter 2.  A Young Athlete

1. Jane Sanderson, "For Garth Brooks, Country Music's Newest Nova, Nashville Proves Sweeter the Second Time Around," *People Weekly,* September 3, 1990, p. 92.

2. Jim Jerome, "The New King of Country," *People Weekly,* October 7, 1991, p. 40.

3. Charles Hirshberg, "He's Garth Brooks, and He's Ready to Speak His Mind," *Life,* July 1992, p. 59.

4. Ibid.

5. Rob Tannenbaum, "Country's New Gold Rush," *Rolling Stone,* April 16, 1992, p. 16.

6. Hirshberg, p. 59.

7. "Garth Brooks," *Current Biography 1992 Annual Cumulation* (New York: H. W. Wilson Co., 1992), p. 80.

8. Jo Sgammato, *American Thunder: The Garth Brooks Story* (New York: Ballantine Books, 1999), p. 13.

9. "Garth Brooks," *Current Biography 1992 Annual Cumulation,* p. 82.

10. "Garth As You've Never Seen Him Before," *Country Weekly,* April 1, 1996, <http://www.planetgarth.com/gbnews/garth020.shtml> (June 29, 2000).

11. Ibid.

12. Scott Schulte, "Garth Brooks: On Success," *Priorities,* Vol. 4, Issue 2, Winter 1999, <http://www.franklincovey.com/priorities/vol4issu2_garth.html> (June 13, 2000).

13. "The Garth Brooks Story," radio interview aired by the Westwood One Network, July 4, 1996, <http://www.planetgarth.com/gbstory.shtml> (April 12, 2000).

14. "Ty England," iMusic Country Showcase, March 2000, <http://imusic.com/showcase/country/tyengland.html> (April 12, 2000).

15. Alanna Nash, "Garth Brooks," *Stereo Review,* April 1992, p. 50.

16. Jerome, p. 44.

17. Bruce Feiler, *Dreaming Out Loud* (New York: Avon Books, 1998), p. 108.

## Chapter 3. Pursuing a Dream

1. Jane Sanderson, "For Garth Brooks, Country Music's Newest Nova, Nashville Proves Sweeter the Second Time Around," *People Weekly,* September 3, 1990, p. 92.

2. Karen Schoemer, "The World According to Garth," *Newsweek,* March 16, 1998, p. 70.

3. Anthony DeCurtis, "Ropin' the Wind: Garth Brooks, the Rolling Stone Interview," *Rolling Stone,* April 1, 1993, p. 34.

4. Sanderson, p. 91.

5. DeCurtis, p. 34.

6. Matt O'Meilia, *Garth Brooks: The Road Out of Santa Fe* (Norman and London: University of Oklahoma Press, 1997), p. 21.

7. Ibid., p. 48.

8. Anne-Marie O'Neill, Beverly Keel, Kelly Williams, and Bob Stewart, "In Pieces," *People Weekly,* October 23, 2000, p. 71.

9. O'Meilia, p. 170.

10. Lisa Gubernick and Peter Newcomb, "The Wal-Mart School of Music," *Forbes,* March 2, 1992, p. 75.

11. Jay Cocks, "Friends in Low Places," *Time,* March 30, 1992, p. 67.

12. Jay Cocks, "Country Classicists," *Time,* September 24, 1990, p. 92.

13. Jo Sgammato, *American Thunder: The Garth Brooks Story* (New York: Ballantine Books, 1999), p. 47.

14. Jimmy Bowen and Jim Jerome, *Rough Mix* (New York: Simon & Schuster, 1997), p. 219.

15. Gerry Wood and Larry Holden, "Garth Rewrites History of Country Music," *Country Weekly,* March 23, 1999, <http://www.countryweekly.com/archives/3_23_99/brooks.htm> (September 1, 1999).

## Chapter 4. The Dance

1. Jo Sgammato, *American Thunder: The Garth Brooks Story* (New York: Ballantine Books, 1999), p. 56.

2. John Wooley, "Here's a few things you may not know about country music's top crooner," *Tulsa World*, July 17, 1997, <http://www.planetgarth.com/gbnews/garth121.html> (February 17, 1999).

3. Ibid.

4. Scott Schulte, "Garth Brooks: On Success," *Priorities*, Vol. 4, Issue 2, Winter 1999, <http://www.franklincovey.com/priorities/vol4issu2_garth.html> (June 13, 2000).

5. "Ty England," iMusic Country Showcase, March 2000, <http://imusic.com/showcase/country/tyengland.html> (April 12, 2000).

6. Jane Sanderson, "For Garth Brooks, Country Music's Newest Nova, Nashville Proves Sweeter the Second Time Around," *People Weekly*, September 3, 1990, p. 91.

7. "Clint Black Led the Way in a Dynamic Decade," *Country Weekly*, June 8, 1999.

8. Jay Cocks, "Country Classicists," *Time*, September 24, 1990, p. 92.

9. Jim Jerome, "The New King of Country," *People Weekly*, October 7, 1991, p. 44.

10. "The Garth Brooks Story," radio interview aired by the Westwood One Network, July 4, 1996, <http://www.planetgarth.com/gbstory/gbstory.shtml> (February 17, 2000).

11. Jerome, p. 44.

12. Gerry Wood and Larry Holden, "Garth Rewrites History of Country Music," *Country Weekly*, March 23, 1999, <http://www.countryweekly.com/archives/3_23_99/brooks.htm> (September 1, 1999).

13. Jimmy Bowen and Jim Jerome, *Rough Mix* (New York: Simon & Schuster, 1997), p. 240.

14. Sanderson, pp. 91–92.

## Chapter 5.  Garth Brooks Fever

1. Don Rhodes, "Brooks' 1990 Augusta concert benefited charity," *Augusta Chronicle,* July 31, 1997, <http://www.planetgarth.com/gbnews/garth203 .shtml> (June 29, 2000).

2. Ibid.

3. Jay Cocks, "Friends In Low Places," *Time,* March 30, 1992, p. 68.

4. Ibid., p. 67.

5. Alanna Nash, "Garth Brooks," *Stereo Review,* April 1992, p. 52.

6. Ibid., p. 50.

7. Rob Tannenbaum, "Country's New Gold Rush," *Rolling Stone,* April 16, 1992, p. 16.

8. "Country Roundup," *Rolling Stone,* April 16, 1992, p. 17.

9. Lisa Gubernick and Peter Newcomb, "The Wal-Mart School of Music," *Forbes,* March 2, 1992, p. 72.

10. Nash, p. 50.

11. Tamara Saviano, "Encore! Garth's tour ends, but he's not disappearing," *Country Weekly,* November 17, 1998, <http://www.country weekly .com/archives/11_17_98/garth.htm> (September 1, 1999).

12. "Garth Brooks," *Current Biography 1992 Annual Cumulation* (New York: H. W. Wilson Co., 1992), p. 85.

13. "The Garth Brooks Story," radio interview aired by the Westwood One Network, July 4, 1996, <http://www.planetgarth.com/gbstory/gbstory .shtml> (February 17, 1999).

14. Jim Jerome, "The New King of Country," *People Weekly,* October 7, 1991, p. 45.

15. Jimmy Bowen and Jim Jerome, *Rough Mix* (New York: Simon & Schuster, 1997), p. 244.

## Chapter 6. The Thunder Rolls

1. Bob Cannon, "It's Over! . . . or Is It?" *Country Weekly,* February 8, 2000, p. 29.

2. "Garth Brooks's Black Eye," *People Weekly,* May 20, 1991, p. 93.

3. Associated Press, "Two Cable Channels Ban a Country Music Video," May 5, 1991, <http://www.planetgarth.com/gbnews/garth104.shtml> (September 1, 1999).

4. "Garth Brooks's Black Eye," p. 93.

5. "The Garth Brooks Story," radio interview aired by the Westwood One Network, July 4, 1996, <http://www.planetgarth.com/gbstory/gbstory.shtml> (February 17, 1999).

6. Lisa Gubernick and Peter Newcomb, "The Wal-Mart School of Music," *Forbes,* March 2, 1992, p. 76.

7. Scott Schulte, "Garth Brooks: On Success," *Priorities,* Vol. 4, Issue 2, Winter 1999, <http://www.franklincovey.com/priorities/vol4issu2_garth.html> (June 13, 2000).

8. "The Garth Brooks Story," radio interview.

9. Alana Nash, "Reviews, Popular Music," *Stereo Review,* November 1991, p. 77.

10. *Country Music People,* June 1990, <http://www.soft.net.uk/stevehoare/kyhint.htm> (September 1, 1999).

11. Gerri Hirshey, "Soul Drain: MOR mega-dweebs Michael Bolton and Garth Brooks are getting rich off the recession blues," *Gentlemen's Quarterly,* June 1992, p. 47.

12. Ibid.

13. "Garth and New Country," *Roughstock's History of Country Music,* <http://www.roughstock.com/history/garthnew.html> (July 10, 2001).

14. Bill Eichenberger, "Brooks' Live Shows Help Explain His Rise to Musical Pantheon," *Columbus Dispatch,* July 24, 1997, <http://www.planetgarth.com/gbnews/garth130.html> (June 29, 2000).

15. "Garth Brooks," *People Weekly,* December 30, 1991, p. 49.

16. Cannon, p. 31.

17. President George H. W. Bush, Remarks at the 25th Anniversary of the Country Music Awards in Nashville, Tennessee, October 3, 1991, <http://bush library.tamu.edu/papers/1991/91100308.html> (June 13, 2000).

18. President George Bush, Proclamation 6358 — Country Music Month, 1991, *Federal Register,* October 15, 1991.

19. Jim Jerome, "The New King of Country," *People Weekly,* October 7, 1991, p. 42.

## Chapter 7. Breaking Records

1. Charles Hirshberg, "He's Garth Brooks . . . And He's Ready to Speak His Mind," *Life,* July 1992, p. 59.

2. Ibid., p. 63.

3. Robert Hilburn, "The Amazing Garth-O-Matic!" *Los Angeles Times,* June 28, 1992, <http:// www.planetgarth.com/gbnews/garth055.shtml> (July 10, 2001).

4. Hirshberg, p. 63.

5. Ibid., p. 62.

6. Clark Staten, "Three Days of Hell in Los Angeles," Emergencynet News Service (ENN), April 29, 1992, <http://www.emergency.com/la-riots.htm> (September 17, 2001).

7. "Major Riot in Los Angeles: 13 Dead, 192 Injured," Emergencynet News Service (ENN), April 30, 1992, <http://www.emergency.com/la-riots.htm> (September 17, 2001).

8. Marjie McCraw, "Garth Brooks: Music's Man," *Ladies Home Journal,* June 1992, p. 44.

9. Karen Schoemer, "The World According to Garth," *Newsweek,* March 16, 1998, p. 70.

10. 1992 Garth Brooks Concert Tour Program.

11. Hilburn, p. 1.

12. Ibid., p. 3.

13. Anthony DeCurtis, "Ropin' the Wind: Garth Brooks, The Rolling Stone Interview," *Rolling Stone,* April 1, 1993, p. 35.

14. Ibid., p. 32.

15. "Don't Be Fooled by Garth Brooks's Flag-Waving," *Interview,* March 1994, p. 47.

16. Ibid.

17. DeCurtis, p. 32.

## Chapter 8. A Night Like Tonight

1. Christopher John Farley, "Trying to Put It Together," *Time,* September 13, 1993, pp. 80–81.

2. Paul Evans, "Review: *In Pieces,*" *Rolling Stone,* October 14, 1993, p. 114.

3. Ibid.

4. Diane Turbide with John Howse, "A Megastar With the Common Touch," *Maclean's,* November 8, 1993, p. 41.

5. Jo Sgammato, *American Thunder: The Garth Brooks Story* (New York: Ballantine Books, 1999), p. 193.

6. Turbide, p. 41.

7. Parke Puterbaugh, "Performance: Garth Brooks," *Rolling Stone,* November 25, 1993, p. 33.

8. Sgammato, pp. 180–181.

9. "Don't Be Fooled by Garth Brooks's Flag-Waving," *Interview,* March 1994, p. 47.

10. Gary Graff, "Garth hops on a fresh horse and hits the road," *Mr. Showbiz Interview,* July 20, 1997, <http://mrshowbiz.go.com/interviews/269_1.html> (April 12, 2000).

11. "Brooks Plays Santa to Family Without a Car," *Deseret News,* January 1, 1994, <http://www.planet garth.com/gbnews/garth030.shtml> (February 17, 1999).

12. Bob Paxman, "Susan Ashton Gets a Boost From a Guy Named Garth," *Country Weekly,* August 16, 1999, <http://www.countryweekly.com/archive/stories/34.html> (June 13, 2000).

13. "Brooks Gets Big Award—and Big Baby," Associated Press, May 4, 1994, <http://www.planet garth.com/gbnews/garth029.shtml> (February 17, 1999).

14. John Schulian, "Ten-Gallon Bozos," *Gentlemen's Quarterly,* June 1994, p. 58.

15. Jim Patterson, "Garth Brooks Knows How to Take 'The Hits,'" Associated Press, February 17, 1995, <http://www.planetgarth.com/gbnews/garth024.shtml> (June 29, 2000).

16. Pamela E. Foster, *My Country: The African Diaspora's Country Music Heritage* (Nashville, Tenn.: My Country, 1998), Foreword.

17. John Marks, "Breaking A Color Line, Song By Song," *U.S. News & World Report,* April 12, 1999, <http://www.usnews.com/usnews/issue/990412/12coun.htm> (July 19, 2000).

18. Rick Overall, "The King of Country—An Inside Look at Superstar Garth Brooks," *Ottawa Sun,* September 1, 1996, <http://www.planetgarth.com/gbnews/garth070/shtml> (June 29, 2000).

19. Richard Harrington, "McDonald's CD Promotions Irk Retailers," *The Washington Post,* October 8, 1994, <http://www.planetgarth.com/gbnews/garth027.shtml> (June 29, 2000).

20. "Garth's Farm Goes to His Head," *Country Weekly,* June 16, 1998, <http://www.planetgarth.com/gbnews/garth227.shtml> (September 1, 1999).

21. Neil Pond, "Garth Gears up for Tour," *Country America,* March 1, 1996, <http://www.planetgarth.com/gbnews/garth018.shtml> (June 29, 2000).

22. Jim Patterson, "Garth Brooks keeps trying to top himself. The country superstar is worried his new album won't be done by Christmas," Associated Press, August 8, 1995.

23. Ibid.

24. David Zimmerman, "Brooks Hoping to Ride 'Horses' Back to the Top," *USA Today,* November 17, 1995, <http://www.planetgarth.com/gbnews/garth006.shtml> (June 29, 2000).

25. Ibid.

26. "The Garth Brooks Story," radio interview aired by the Westwood One Network, July 4, 1996, <http://www.planetgarth.com/gbstory/gbstory.shtml> (February 17, 1999).

27. Bruce Feiler, *Dreaming Out Loud* (New York: Avon Books, 1998), p. 10.

28. "Garth Brooks walks away with top honor, not award," Garth Brooks' "acceptance" speech at the AMA, <http://www.planetgarth.com/gbnews/garthaward.html> (June 29, 2000).

## Chapter 9.  A Charitable Heart

1. "Brooks Searches for Match to Light Sales of New Album," *USA Today,* March 6, 1996, <http://www.planetgarth.com/gbnews/garth002.shtml> (June 29, 2000).

2. Dave Schwensen, "Garth Brooks Triumphs Review & Interview," *The Morning Journal,* March 1996, p. 2, <http://www.thecomedybook.com/Archives/garth_brooks.htm> (April 12, 2000).

3. "Garth Speaks About Education," *Country Weekly,* March 26, 1996, <http://www.planetgarth.com/gbnews/garth009.shmtl> (February 17, 1999).

4. Schwensen, p. 4.

5. "Garth Thanks His Fans," Associated Press, July 23, 1996, <http://www.planetgarth.com/gbnews/garth059.shtml> (June 29, 2000).

6. Scott Schulte, "Garth Brooks: On Success," *Priorities,* Vol. 4, Issue 2, Winter 1999, <http://www.franklincovey.com/priorities/vol4issu2_garth.html> (June 13, 2000).

7. Ibid.

8. "The Garth Brooks Story," radio interview aired by the Westwood One Network, July 4, 1996, <http://www.planetgarth.com/gbstory/gbstory.shtml> (February 17, 1999).

9. "Wishing On a Star," *Telegraph Journal,* October 5, 1996, <http://www.planetgarth.com/gbnews/garth079.shtml> (June 29, 2000).

10. Neil Pond, "Garth Gears Up for Tour," *Country America,* March 1, 1996, p. 2, <http://www.planetgarth.com/gbnews/garth018.shtml> (June 29, 2000).

11. "Garth Brooks Surprises Two Millionth Ticket Buyers in Charleston," Press Release, February 17, 1997, <http://www.planetgarth.com/gbnews/garth088.shtml> (June 29, 2000).

12. Jenny Smedley, *Ripples* (Norwich, England: Third Floor Productions, 1998), p. 259.

13. Bruce Feiler, *Dreaming Out Loud* (New York: Avon Books, 1998), p. 107.

14. Mark Lasswell, "Garth Takes Manhattan," *TV Guide,* August 2, 1997, p. 33.

15. Christopher John Farley, "Garth Brooks Unplugged," *Time,* August 18, 1997, p. 66.

16. Jack Hurst, "Friends in Some Places," *Chicago Tribune,* October 19, 1997, <http://www.planetgarth.com/gbnews/garth160.html> (June 29, 2000).

17. Karen Schoemer, "The World According to Garth," *Newsweek,* March 16, 1998, p. 68.

18. "Garth Brooks," *Rolling Stone,* August 7, 1997, <http://www.rollingstone.com/sections/news> (April 12, 2000).

19. Gary Graff, "Garth Hops on a Fresh Horse and Hits the Road," *Mr. Showbiz Interview,* <http://mrshowbiz.go.com/interviews/269_1.html> (April 12, 2000).

20. "Garth and Trisha to Release Duet "In Another's Eyes" on Yearwood's Upcoming MCA Album," Entertainment Wire, August 13, 1997, <http://www.planetgarth.com/gbnews/garth139 .html> (June 29, 2000).

21. Ibid.

22. "MCA Records Releases Special Live Audio Mix of Duet Exclusively to Radio," PRN Newswire, September 26, 1997, <http://www.planetgarth.com/ gbnews/garth154.html> (June 29, 2000).

23. "Garth Brooks Celebrates 3 Million with Style in Lincoln, Neb.," Entertainment Wire, September 29, 1997, <http://www.planetgarth.com/gbnews/ garth155.html> (June 29, 2000).

24. Thom Geier, "Country's Riding in the Saddle, But Not So High," *U.S. News & World Report,* November 17, 1997, p. 75.

25. "Randy Travis Succeeds Amid Country's Changes," *Country Weekly,* February 2, 1998.

26. Richard Corliss, "Can Garth Save Country?" *Time,* December 15, 1997, pp. 130–131.

27. Feiler, p. 180.

## Chapter 10.  New Faces

1. Tom Krasovic, "Padres as Thrilled by Garth Brooks' Fantasy Fling as He Is," *San Diego Union-Tribune,* March 16, 1998, <http://www.planet garth.com/gbnews/garth210.shtml> (February 17, 1999).

2. John Blanchette, "Golf May Not be Brooks' Game, but He's a Hit on Course," *The Spokesman-Review,* July 28, 1998, <http://www.spokane.net:80/ news-story-body.asp?Date=072898&ID> (September 1, 1999).

3. Larry Holden, "Garth's Hope Floats Hit Joins Country, Hollywood," *Country Weekly,* August 11, 1998, <http://www.countryweekly.com/archive/dated_stories/3_11_98/garth.html> (June 13, 2000).

4. Gary Graff, "Okie Dokie," *Rolling Stone,* November 12, 1998.

5. John Foyston, "The World According to Garth," *The Oregonian,* November 13, 1998, <http://www.oregonlive.com/cgi-bin/printer/printer.cgi> (June 28, 2000).

6. Christopher John Farley and David E. Thigpen, "Super Tuesday!" *Time,* November 23, 1998, p. 104.

7. "Garth Brooks Double Live: Over One Million Copies Sold in One Week," Press Release, November 25, 1998, <http://www.planetgarth.com/gbnews/garth298.shtml> (February 17, 1999).

8. Tamara Saviano, "Encore! Garth's Tour Ends, but He's Not Disappearing," *Country Weekly,* November 17, 1998, <http://www.countryweekly.com/archives/11_17_98/garth.htm> (September 1, 1999).

9. E. J. McGregor, "Garth Brooks's Latest Hit," CNN/Sports Illustrated: CIGNA Special Adventure— The Power of Caring, September 24, 1999, <http://www.cnnsi.com/caring/brooks.html> (April 12, 2000).

10. Mike Klis, "At the Plate, Garth Brooks Goes Hitless," *Denver Post,* March 21, 1999, <http://www.planetgarth.com/gbnews/garth331.shtml> (September 1, 1999).

11. "Brooks' Foundation a Hit with Big Leaguers— and Kids," ESPN, January 15, 1999, <http://www.planetgarth.com/gbnews/garth303.shtml> (February 17, 1999).

12. "Garth Brooks Hopes for More Hits in Tryout with Padres," Associated Press, February 12, 1999, <http://www.planetgarth.com/gbnews/garth304 .shtml> (February 17, 1999).

13. Bob Nightengale, "Good Old Country Hardball," *USA Today—Baseball Weekly,* March 18, 1999, <http://www.planetgarth.com/gbnews/ garth323.shtml> (September 1, 1999).

14. "White Sox Defeat Padres but Garth Gets a Single," Associated Press, March 21, 1999, <http://www.planetgarth.com/gbnews/garth326 .shtml> (September 1, 1999).

15. Gerry Wood, "The Two Faces of Garth," *Country Weekly,* August 31, 1999, p. 20.

16. Ibid.

17. Eric Boehlert, "The Non-Life of Chris Gaines," *Rolling Stone,* November 16, 1999, <http://www .rollingstone.com/sections/news . . . > (April 12, 2000).

18. Kieran Grant, "It's Chris, er, Garth Speaking," *Toronto Sun,* September 9, 1999, <http://www.canoe .com/JamCountryBrooks/sep9_garth.html> (July 24, 2000).

19. Bob Paxman, "Tug of War," *Country Weekly,* September 5, 2000, p. 41.

20. Ibid., p. 30.

21. "Garth Brooks into the Sunset?" *E!Online News,* December 15, 1999, <http://www.lycos.com/ cgi-bin/pursuit?quer . . . > (June 28, 2000).

22. Anne-Marie O'Neill, Beverly Keel, Kelly Williams, and Bob Stewart, "In Pieces," *People Weekly,* October 23, 2000, p. 71.

23. Bob Paxman, "Midlife Crisis," *Country Weekly,* May 15, 2001, p. 39.

24. "How Serious Is Garth Brooks about Retirement?" *Wall Street,* AP Worldstream, November 2, 2000, <http://ehostvgw17.epnet.com> (May 1, 2001).

25. Russ DeVault, "Don't Bet the Farm on Garth Brooks' Retirement," *The Atlanta Journal and Constitution,* November 5, 2000, p. L6.

26. Wood, p.22.

27. Kevin C. Johnson, "Country Music May Survive A.G.: (After Garth)," *St. Louis Post-Dispatch,* November 12, 2000, p. C3.

28. Diane Samms Rush, "Garth Brooks turns the Spotlight on Others at Gala Party," Knight-Ridder/Tribune News Service, November 3, 2000, <http://www.elibrary.com> (May 1, 2001).

29. Jim Patterson, "Garth Brooks Releases 'Scarecrow,'"Associated Press, <http://news.excite.com/printstory/news/ap/011114/13/ent-wkd-nashville-sound-garth-brook> (November 13, 2001).

30. Ibid.

# Further Reading

Howey, Paul. *Garth Brooks: Chart Bustin' Country.* Minneapolis, Minn.: Lerner Publications, 1997.

Sgammato, Jo. *American Thunder: The Garth Brooks Story.* New York: Ballantine Books, 1999.

Uscher, Mitchell. *Garth Brooks: Hitting the High Notes.* Kansas City, Mo.: Andrews McMeel Publishing, 1999.

## Internet Addresses

**Unofficial Garth Brooks web site**
<http://www.planetgarth.com>

**News, songs, bio, video**
<http://www.troyal-garth-brooks.org>

**Career chronology, essays**
<http://www.roughstock.com/garth>

**Photos, news, concert information**
<http://www.garthbrooks.com>

# Index

Page numbers for photographs are in **boldface** type.